KU-266-262

WHEN YOUR CHILD NEEDS HELP

LEEDS BE

Leeds Metropolitan University

17 0507878 2

When Your Child Needs Help

Norma Doft, Ph.D.,
with *Barbara Aria*

Crown Trade Paperbacks/New York

This book is dedicated to Leah Levinger,
who has dedicated her life to understanding children, and to sharing
that understanding with others.

LEEDS METROPOLITAN
UNIVERSITY
LIBRARY

1705078782
AJ-B
CC-95427
5.6.08
618.928914 OOL

This book is illustrated throughout with case studies from my clinical practice.
To protect their privacy, all names of parents and children have been
changed, as have any details that might identify them

Copyright © 1992 by Norma Doft, Ph.D., and Barbara Aria

All rights reserved. No part of this book many be reproduced or transmitted in
any form or by any means, electronic or mechanical, including photocopying,
recording, or by any information storage and retrieval system, without
permission in writing from the publisher.

Published by Crown Publishers, Inc., 201 East 50th Street, New York, New
York 10022. Member of the Crown Publishing Group.

Random House, Inc. New York, Toronto, London, Sydney, Auckland

CROWN TRADE PAPERBACKS and colophon are trademarks of Crown
Publishers, Inc.

Manufactured in the United States of America

Library of Congress Cataloging-in-Publication Data

Doft, Norma.
When your child needs help: a parent's guide to therapy for children / Norma
Doft with Barbara Aria. —
p. cm.
Originally published: New York : Harmony Books, © 1992.
Includes index.
1. Child psychotherapy. 2. Adjustment disorders in children — Diagnosis.
3. Parenting. I. Aria, Barbara. II. Title.
[RJ504.D58 1994]   93-43805
618.92' 8914 — dc20   CIP

ISBN 0-517-881691
BVG 01

ACKNOWLEDGMENTS

I would like to thank all the parents who have allowed me to bring their stories to other parents, and particularly those who were willing to be interviewed for this book. I'm sure that anyone reading about their experiences with child therapy will have felt enlightened by the insights they have to offer.

My gratitude also to Madeleine Morel, my agent, on whose impetus this book began life, and to all those at Crown who helped the book come to completion—in particular, Harriet Bell, my first editor, who believed in and committed herself to the project; Peter Guzzardi, my second editor, who gave this book its breadth and shape; and John Michel, who took over the editing of this book in its final stages and fine-tuned the text.

I am deeply indebted to Martin Doft, M.D., Zina Steinberg, Ph.D., and Susan Warshaw, Ph.D., who read the manuscript and offered many valuable suggestions. I would also like to acknowledge my debt to Stella Chess, M.D. and her husband, Alexander Thomas, M.D., whose life's work, clarifying the role of innate temperament, has informed my work and this book.

Finally, my thanks to Barbara Aria, my cowriter.

CONTENTS

Foreword   *ix*

Preface   *xi*

1. DOES MY CHILD NEED HELP?   *1*
   The Dilemma
   Understanding Child Development
   Growing Pains—Normal
   Snags in Development
   A Cry For Help? Knowing the Signs
   Typical Childhood Problems
   Children to Watch

2. THE CONSULTATION: FINDING A GOOD FIT   *50*
   The First Parent Visit
   The Child Visits
   The Second Parent Visit
   The One-Time Preventative Consultation

3. A LOOK THROUGH THE WINDOW: PLAY THERAPY   *74*
   What Is Play Therapy?
   Why Play?

How Children Use Play for Emotional Health
Play in Therapy
What Goes On in the Therapy Room?
How the Therapist Hopes to Help the Child
Developing Self-Esteem

4. PARENT-WORK   *118*

What Is Parent-Work?
What Forms Can Parent-Work Take?
How Can the Child Therapist Help Parents Deal With
Troublesome Feelings?
How Parent-Work Helps You to Help Your Child
Making the Most of Parent Sessions
Parents' Rights and Responsibilities

5. PROGRESS, REGRESS, AND GOOD-BYES   *159*

The Phases of Treatment
Regression—Two Steps Forward, One Step Back
Evaluating Your Child's Progress
Saying Good-Bye

6. PARENTS SPEAK   *185*

APPENDIX A: SHOPPING FOR THERAPY   *205*

APPENDIX B: OTHER FORMS OF THERAPY   *211*

INDEX   *217*

FOREWORD

Psychological help for children—or, as it is usually called, "therapy for children"—has acquired a certain mystique. In some circles, child therapy is almost a fad, to be used as a badge of honor. Other parents react to the suggestion as if it were an accusation, a statement that their child is thought to be crazy. And indeed, there are therapists, whether psychiatrists or those without a medical degree, who find a clinical diagnosis for every child who comes for evaluation and automatically recommend long-term psychoanalytic treatment.

Children's fears, uncertainties, periods of troublesome belligerence, confused ideas, and many more such happenings can mean, like stumbling in walking, anything from a crack in the sidewalk to a deep problem requiring professional help. The same is true with childhood psychological problems.

If child therapy is decided upon, its nature should vary with the degree and nature of the problem. Children are highly individual, and interventions to help must be also individually designed to fit.

I am a child psychiatrist once considered to be a maverick in my field, surprisingly, for espousing some of the very points made in this book—especially those concerning temperament. I read Norma Doft's *When Your Child Needs Help* very carefully, and to my great pleasure, I have found her book full of good, common sense in addition to showing an excellent mastery of the concepts and scientific work in our field. As a guide to therapy for children, this book is most useful to parents. It covers common questions and doubts, explains how various therapies proceed, explains both confidentiality and the parent-therapist collegial relationship.

Such a book will be most useful for today's parents.

Stella Chess, M.D.
PROFESSOR OF CHILD PSYCHIATRY,
NEW YORK UNIVERSITY
MEDICAL CENTER

PREFACE

This book began life as a parent's guide to child therapy—a guide for those who are anxious about a child and struggling with the question of whether professional help is needed; for those who are considering finding help but aren't sure how to start looking; and for those whose children are already in therapy but so often feel shut out of the therapy process by the important rule of confidentiality. If you are one of these parents, this book may provide you with a look through the window into the therapy room. It's really not such a mysterious place when you get to know it. In fact, by opening a window and offering you a glimpse of how I play and work with children, I hope I'll be able to offer some insights into the links between a child's mental processes, emotions, and sometimes baffling behaviors—insights that can help every parent better understand their child.

Often parents tell me that I know their children better than they do, but in fact parents know their children best. Although I may have certain psychological insights that I can communicate to parents in order to help them understand their children in new ways and so adapt their styles of parenting to a child's unique needs, I also learn a great deal about children from their parents. It's because of this two-way process of learning that I consider parents' work one of the most essential elements in play therapy. And it's for this reason also that I hope this book will allow you to take a look through the window and get a feel for what goes on in child treatment. The parent who truly understands the process is going to be a far more effective collaborator in the treatment of his or her child.

But this book is more than just a guide, and more than a book for parents considering or involved in the process of child therapy. It is a book about children and their feelings. It speaks through the medium of "play therapy," because play is a child's most natural language, and because play therapy is the tool that for many years has allowed me to be helpful to children. It's a wonderful tool, as broad in scope as one cares to make it; a tool that relates to the everyday lives of children. What you'll find in these pages comes from my personal experience as a play therapist, and it reflects my style of working—a flexible style informed by thirty years of working with all kinds of children and incorporating many different techniques.

Although children of all ages can need help, I decided to focus in this book on therapy for the child of eleven and under. I see treatment of adolescents as an entirely different field, one that no longer involves play therapy. These older children can talk and think on a level that allows them to use the mode of adults, even though some of their issues—such as separating from parents, and self-esteem—aren't so different from the issues that younger children bring to my office.

This book tells the stories of children who came to me deeply troubled and in pain, but who, like all children, had strengths with which I could help them. It tells about how I worked with these children, using play and language to help them reveal and resolve those feelings that were invading their lives and making them so unhappy. Their feelings were not so different from the feelings that many children have at one time or another. Their reactions to life's stesses and demands were intense but on some level very common, and you may well recognize aspects of your own child in these accounts. In reading about these children, how I helped them, and how I helped their parents to help them, you might find some insights into how you can help your not-so-stuck child more easily tackle the inevitable snags of growing up.

Along with the children's stories, I also tell about their parents, many of whom came to me anxious, confused, and aching with the idea that they had somehow failed their children. Every parent struggles to some extent with these feelings of guilt and shame. Part of my work as a child therapist, and part of my intention in this book, is to help you see how so many factors beyond a parent's control influence a child's development. Of course, parenting *is* a factor, too, and is often confused by voices from one's own childhood or by abstract ideas about what kind of parent you want to be; perhaps the stories in these pages will give you some new ways of looking at yourself as a parent, and at the very important issue of what kind of parent your child needs you to be.

WHEN YOUR CHILD NEEDS HELP

1

DOES MY CHILD NEED HELP?

Mr. and Mrs. Baker sat in my office looking exhausted but hopeful, and began to tell me about their daughter, Stephanie, and about their battles with and around this child. As they talked, Mrs. Baker grew almost teary-eyed while she tried to describe her daughter's pain. Mr. Baker was more reserved, but obviously full of despair over the effect that Stephanie's recent behavior was having on the family and on their marriage. They were both desperately worried and frustrated over a little girl whom they both loved dearly, but they each saw the problem differently, and this was creating conflict and tension between them.

Stephanie had always been a shy child, they said, reluctant to venture beyond the safety of her mother's watchful eye. Now she was almost six, and while they could see that other children her age were gaining in independence, Stephanie remained overly cautious about the world outside her home. She clung to her mother, who I could sense understood her daughter's reticence to meet the world because she, too, seemed a little shy.

Stephanie's shyness was not really the problem, and neither was school. According to Mr. and Mrs. Baker, Stephanie's teacher in school described her as quiet and unassertive; she was excessively accommodating to the other kids, seldom gave rein to her feelings or imagination, and seemed at a loss for what to do during free time. It was hard to imagine this quiet, undemanding little girl ever raising her voice or putting up a fight.

But at home Stephanie was tyrannical. She demanded her way in almost everything, fought her parents with screams and tantrums, and demanded rigid routines. She insisted on her right to make important decisions about her life; she decided, for instance, that day camp was definitely not for her and spent the entire summer by choice stuck in the apartment. Sundays, said Mr. Baker, were the worst of all. He felt that Sundays should be family days, when they could all enjoy doing things together or visit friends and relatives. But inevitably there were battles. Stephanie refused to leave the house for family trips or visits, and so they couldn't go; she was too big now just to pick up and load into the car.

"Everything ends up being so unhappy," said Mr. Baker. Instead of Sundays being happy family days, the whole family would end up fighting.

"But how could I force her to go?" asked Mrs. Baker. Her instincts led her to soothe and protect her daughter, because she knew there were fears, whereas her husband saw Stephanie as more overindulged than frightened—a child who got her way at everyone else's expense. "We have to have a life," he insisted.

Stephanie's parents looked anguished, sitting across the room from me and telling me what their lives had become. Obviously, the whole family was stuck, and the whole family was suffering. Through her fears, Stephanie had been controlling their lives for months, turning their home into a domestic war zone.

Stephanie's mother told me that she had never worried much over her daughter's shyness in school—after all, Stephanie never got into trouble. But as her home behavior became increasingly intolerable, it was straining the relationship between her husband and herself. Naturally, they argued about how best to deal with Stephanie, and as the tension between them mounted, both felt increasingly overwhelmed by the situation, and both felt drained of the energy that Stephanie's behavior demanded of them.

Meanwhile, an increasingly miserable Stephanie, whose uncomfortable feelings were now compounded by the sense that she had become a problem for her parents, was not getting any less angry or any less shy. Yet it wasn't until Stephanie's aunt said to Mrs. Baker, "Don't you think there's something really wrong here?" that Stephanie's mother sought professional help.

Therapy, or a Good Spanking?

You might feel that all a child like Stephanie needs is a good spanking. Her parents *could* have spanked her, or yelled at her, but that would have just made her feel more frightened, more weak, and she never would have grown. She would have felt totally annihilated by her family, by the only thing that felt safe to her at this point.

Besides the work I needed to do with Stephanie in treatment concerning her problems with separation and her feeling of weakness, it *was* critical that I help her parents learn to set good limits in order to help Stephanie move along. All children need firm, clear, and consistent limits in their lives. Although there had been some limits on this girl's behavior, her parents had disagreed between themselves on what was acceptable behavior from their daughter, and her mother often backed down from a "no"; in other words, the limits weren't set consistently. Because she was indulged so much by her mother (her father was stricter), she felt entitled to do what she wanted, and no demand was made on her to overcome her fears.

It wasn't simply a matter of making Stephanie obedient, it was a matter of helping her feel stronger. Clear and consistent limits weren't the whole story, but they were a part of it, and I should point out that they worked because Stephanie knew that her parents genuinely cared about her and had her best interests in mind. When she did something because a limit had been set by a firm though caring parent, she developed an internal control as a result and felt stronger, less babylike: "Mother says I can't, therefore I will resist doing this," as opposed to "They're going to kill me, so I'd better not."

THE DILEMMA—DOES MY CHILD NEED HELP?

How can you know when your child's in pain? At times when he proves difficult, do you just need to be more strict or more gentle with him, or is there some underlying problem that's affecting his behavior? Or is it a combination of the two? And how can you tell the difference between a child who's simply having a difficult few weeks and a child who's really troubled? Every parent knows that children go through all sorts of difficult phases in their lives. When trouble arises, there's always the hope that your child will suddenly return to normal, the problem having gone away by itself as others have in the past.

Few parents survive their children's growing years without periods of struggle. Whether it's over giving up a diaper, or over eating, whether it's about letting you leave him with the baby-sitter in the morning, or about going to sleep at night, or because he's hitting other children, these struggles with your child can make you anxious, angry, exasperated, and bewildered. How long will it go on? Is this normal?

All children have their emotional ups and downs, and

sooner or later they emerge from the difficult phase. But sometimes, when nothing you do makes any difference to your child's behavior or mood and the whole family is feeling the strain, it seems as if your struggles might go on forever. It saddens you to see your child in pain; it might even anger you to feel that he's trying to make your life difficult.

This is the point at which many parents begin to ask themselves: What's the matter with my child? Why is he acting like this? Am I doing something wrong, or could I do something more to change things? Am I just a worrier, or is there something wrong here? And finally, does my child need help?

Knowing that no two children are the same makes the decision even more difficult; what might be symptomatic of an emotional conflict in one six-year-old could, in another child of the same age, be no more than a normal stumbling over some innate aspect of his personality, or it could be simply immaturity. How can you tell whether your three-year-old is on the road to being toilet trained and is just taking a little bit longer than other children, or if in fact there's some emotional roadblock that has to be removed? And how long do you wait and see? Although parents know that children all develop at different rates, and have different vulnerabilities, it's easy to worry.

If your child is very young, it can be especially hard to figure out what's happening. Pre-schoolers are going through so many changes—every couple of months there's a new development, a new problem, a new characteristic. When a child is older it's much easier to say, "This has been going on for a long time" or "Things don't seem to be right, he's never been like this before."

Many parents understand that certain factors, such as family problems, can seriously upset a child. It's only normal. But how do you know when your child's reaction is beyond the realm of normality, especially if your other child takes things in his stride? How long can you expect your child to grieve over

Grandpa's death, or to desperately miss the nanny who cared for him since he was a few weeks old? What kinds of reactions are normal when a child is faced with divorce? What about the child who meets tragedy with an "I don't care" response—is that normal?

Perhaps your child seems to be doing fine in his life at home, but his teacher says he's out of control; or, as in Stephanie's case, the child is out of control at home but a cautious, well-behaved little student. What's the meaning of this? Parents whose children are good in school often don't worry so much about the problems at home, but as Stephanie's case shows, even the classroom angel can really be in pain. Other parents, whose children don't seem to be having any problems at home but whose teachers complain about their behavior in school, might say, "It's the teacher's fault. She doesn't know how to control her class." How can you tell where the problem really lies?

These are some of the issues I'll try to deal with during the course of this chapter. Of course, I can't address every likelihood, and I can't tell you whether or not your child in particular needs help—that decision can only be made after a consultation with a therapist, based on her recommendations—but there are signals that you as a parent can listen for, and there are guidelines that can help you to distinguish between appropriate upsets and problems deserving the attention of a professional.

Parents know their children better than anyone and can usually sense when some negative mood or behavior is beyond the usual, or when the usual feels too burdensome for child and family. Trust in your intuition, talk to his teachers, step back from the fights and the worries and think about it in a calm moment. Think about your expectations for your child—are they reasonable, or are you expecting him to be more mature than he is capable of being at his age? Look at the other children he plays with in school or in the park. Sometimes, for example, parents decide that their child is behaving intolerably because they themselves have a low tolerance for noise or mess.

The guidelines later in this chapter will help you think about the problem constructively. But first, to help you better understand what's happening in your child's life and to place his behavior in perspective, let me begin by talking some more about the kinds of demands that growing up entails, and why at certain times it's perfectly normal for your child to behave in ways that might worry or annoy you.

UNDERSTANDING CHILD DEVELOPMENT

Childhood is a very short time of great changes. Those changes are built into the process of growing up, but for a small person with limited experience and many natural anxieties, they're never easy.

Areas of Development

A growing child is developing in three main areas. In one area we see the development of a sense of self, and its important offshoot, the development of self-esteem. This begins with the baby's realization that "I am me, everyone else is not me," and a little later, "I'm a girl, he's a boy," and grows increasingly complex, so that the seven-year-old can look at himself in several different contexts and has a many-faceted sense of self.

Another area of growth is in the ability to form attachments and relationships. This begins as the dependent infant forms an attachment to his parents, allowing himself to be comforted, and learns that the world is a safe and nurturing place in which his needs will be met. If all goes well and the child has learned to trust in the world around him, by the age of eight or nine he's able to have different kinds of important relationships outside the family.

The third area of development involves the learning of cognitive, physical, and social skills. Between the time when a baby learns to grasp, to talk, to yield to society's first demand that he give up his diaper, and a little later to share and take turns, and the time when, as a nine-year-old, he's able to cross the street, visit his best friend, and help him with his homework, many tasks have to be learned. In a few short years, he has grown from an entirely dependent, entirely egocentric infant into an almost independent and, ideally, empathetic individual.

How Children Get Stuck in Their Development

Children have to master a huge number of tasks in each of these three areas in order to develop normally. If a child has difficulties in any one area, it makes it harder for him to move on, as other areas may also be affected. As a baby, he has to learn to see himself as physically and emotionally separate from his mother so that he can tolerate separating from her. The harder it is for him to separate, the harder it will be to comfortably go to school or to go play at a friend's house. In such a situation, he's miserably scared a lot of the time that he's going to be left somewhere or with someone, and angry at himself and the world every time he's stuck sitting with Mom on the park bench, watching other kids play together in the sand. Every area of development is being affected—he's stuck until he learns that he can function separately and safely away from his mother.

Parents sometimes consult me because their children are, developmentally, lagging behind others of the same age. I usually tell them that as long as the child keeps moving, even if he's always lagging a few months behind the other children he plays with, then there's probably no need to worry. He'll get there in time. It's only when a child stops growing in one or more areas, and it's not just a resting period, that he might be stuck.

What do I mean by stuck? Let me tell you about a five-year-old child, brought to me because for the past year she had been having terrible problems playing with children her own age. Up until that point she had been a very popular kid—in fact, her good ideas had made her something of a leader—but now nobody wanted to play with her anymore.

What had happened was that this little girl had reached the age when children can quite happily play *with* others rather than just alongside them. Her friends had learned to share, to take turns, and to cooperate with one another, and they expected other children to do the same. But this girl's fierce need to control things made it impossible for her to play cooperatively, or to compromise, and the other children didn't want to deal with her bossiness. At the same time, she was too young to understand why children were calling her "bossy," or why other kids were giving up on her. She ended up playing by herself, and therefore she was denied the social experiences that would have helped her to learn how to play cooperatively; she was stuck in her social development.

GROWING PAINS—
NORMAL SNAGS IN DEVELOPMENT

All parents know that children have their hard times and their easy times, and that it's not necessary to run to a therapist every time there's a problem. When your child starts having tantrums all over the place, or complains sullenly that none of his friends will play with him anymore, your first response is to say, "It's just a phase" or "It's just because he's still getting used to being in school all day." And you're probably right (although, of course, you would still want to try helping the unhappy child to work through his upset, just as you would want to set limits on the behavior of a child going through a tantrumy phase).

Life is stressful for children, and these stresses can lead them to behave in all sorts of ways that, while perhaps not welcome, are absolutely normal. Most of the time they manage to pick themselves back up and keep going. In fact, most of the difficult times in childhood are just normal snags.

My point is that mental health is not the absence of stress—it's the capacity to master stressful situations and to move on developmentally. Childhood stress can be related to development itself, or it might have to do with other things that are going on in the child's life. First of all, let's look at the stresses a child faces simply by virtue of being a developing individual.

The Developmental Seesaw

As you watch your child grow, you might notice that every now and again he seems to go through a period when he's unusually upset or at a loss, and that these periods are often followed by some new milestone in his development. Especially when he's very young and growing fast, life with him can seem like a continuous series of ups and downs.

Many developmental psychologists see development as an alternating pattern of equilibrium and disequilibrium, almost like a seesaw. When the child has mastered a new stage in his growing up, he feels a sense of internal order and calm. But as he meets each new developmental task, he is thrown off balance, and calm is replaced by turbulence. For example, for a period of time your two-year-old has been busy developing a sense of himself as separate from his mother. Finally he has it all figured out: "We're two different people—I can leave and return, and she'll still be there. She, too, goes away and comes back." Everything seems to be quiet and then, over the next few months, things are thrown into turmoil again as the child—now able to separate physically and emotionally from his mother and therefore to take a broader view of the world—discovers his father in a new and deeper way. Suddenly his picture of life becomes complicated. Where there was a safe package of two—the dependent child and his mother—now there's an untidy triangle of three. The dependence-separateness issue may have been resolved, but now there are new issues confronting him. There are rivalries, feelings of being left out, feelings of being less safely cared for than he once thought. He may be confused, frustrated, and a little overwhelmed as he struggles with this new phase. But eventually, as he reorganizes his internal world to make room for his new perceptions and the tasks required of him, he's able to function smoothly again on a new and more advanced level.

Turbulent Times

The "terrible twos" (as in later years adolescence) is the most familiar of these difficult phases in childhood. Although you may think your toddler is just out to give you a hard time, his frequent tantrums and refusals are developmentally necessary because they allow him to experience and assert himself as separate from you—"You say no, I say yes, therefore we're two different people." This is a stressful period, both for you and for your child, but once that separateness is established, relative calm is restored.

Less familiar are the "aggressive threes," when children are first expected to play harmoniously alongside others. They're out of their diapers, they're quite verbal, and it's hard to think of them as toddlers anymore—so how come little Johnny keeps yanking Eric's pail away from him? Why doesn't he ask for it and wait his turn, rather than struggle with his friend? And how come your little girl's been hitting the kid who won't give up her doll, only to have her hair pulled by the doll's rightful owner? The answer is that children of this age are in a transitional phase—they're mature enough to talk to one another and follow simple game plans, and they know that they're not supposed to hit or bite, but they don't yet have the social skills that will let them include another person, to tolerate frustration, or to wait for their turn. It's a time of disequilibrium until—through

LEEDS METROPOLITAN UNIVERSITY LIBRARY

these kinds of social interactions—they learn to play with one another.

Sometimes difficult times happen in preparation for, or in reaction to, developments (rather than for the sake of development, as in the terrible twos). A child who has an intense resistance to toilet training might regress as a way of assuring himself that he can still be babied occasionally, even though using the potty makes him a big boy. As your two-year-old makes his first steps out into the world, crossing the room away from you or going to play in the sand while you wait on the bench, he has to run back periodically to restore his sense of security. In one sense he's ready to separate from you—and wants to—yet emotionally he's pulled in the other direction because he still feels a powerful need to be near you.

These conflicts can make him feel frustrated and anxious. One part of him says, "Wouldn't it be nice to stay a baby, to be safely cuddled and rocked and loved?" while the other part says, "If I use the potty, I'll be a big boy like Daddy, and Mommy and Daddy will smile and be happy." He might also be receiving conflicting messages from within the family; although his mother's proud of every step he takes in his growing up, perhaps she also looks a little wistfully on these signs of vanishing babyhood. He has to resolve these conflicts before he can move on; in the meantime, you can expect some trouble.

Other Common Sources of Snags— Childhood Stress

Children have to deal not only with normal, phase-related stress, but also with certain factors in their lives over which they have no control. The most obvious are events that happen in the family. Parents divorce, a sibling is born, Mom gets sick, Daddy has to go away on a long trip, a big sister leaves home—these can provoke periods when the child seems out of sorts. He might be angry or withdrawn, he might be restless and unable to concentrate in school, he might be disobedient or fearful, but most of the time the troubles pass and life returns to normal.

What are the other main sources of stress in childhood, besides external factors? I would say, the child's temperament, certain constitutional factors, and his personal world of meaning—in other words, how he interprets the world around him.

External or Traumatic Events. Things that happen in children's lives can have a huge impact on their levels of stress. Hurricanes and earthquakes are obvious examples on the large scale. Robberies and accidents can be quite upsetting, and family events such as divorce or death are high on the stress list. Other common, stressful events include the birth of a sibling, beginning school or even a new class, financial problems in the family, or a mother returning to work. I'll talk about the most stressful of these later, when I discuss children who should be watched for the possibility of emotional difficulties.

Of course, you can help children deal with events that you feel might be upsetting or stressful. The main thing is to make it clear to the child that you are there to listen to whatever he wants to talk about, however painful the subject, and that his thoughts won't make you uncomfortable. Also, although parents sometimes think they can help their child by not dwelling on a frightening or upsetting incident, I find that children really do need some acknowledgment of the fact that what they have experienced is, indeed, unusually scary for them and that you can understand their being upset. Basically, you need to give the child two messages: "Yes, it was scary. But it's over now and you're safe."

Stress From Positive Events. Because children tend to cherish the familiar, even change on the most positive level—a new house, summer vacation, Grandma's visit—can be quite stressful. Some children can become impossible in the days (or even weeks) leading up to some special event; birthdays are the obvious example. Excitement overload can take a toll, and leave a child weepy or irritable; you might even think your child's very upset about something, but it soon passes as things calm down, or as the long-awaited event is behind him.

Temperament

There is huge diversity in human life, with variations in temperament often showing up from birth. Children can be very adaptive to change or rigidly attached to routine; they can be aggressive or shy; intense in their reactions or easygoing and low-key; prone to mood swings or even-tempered. Even many children who seem like "problems" are somewhere on the continuum of normal variation.

Certain kinds of temperament make life a more stressful experience. The most obvious are a very shy temperament, and what's known as a "difficult" temperament. Shy children can use a little help from their parents in learning to cope with rather than avoid new situations. The girl who turns down an invitation to a birthday party because she's scared she won't know any of the other children is bound to feel very angry and disappointed in herself. The more opportunities and pleasures missed, the more that anger and disappointment build up. But if she can learn that new situations are only "new" (uncomfortable) for a short time, then she'll gradually learn to hang in there.

Children who can be described as "difficult" from birth usually need some special kinds of attention for things to go well. I'll be talking about them later in this chapter when I discuss "Children to Watch."

Constitutional Factors

A child's potential is largely affected by his mental and physical makeup. Some kinds of makeup can make certain situations quite stressful. A child with high energy levels, for instance, may have difficulties in a traditional classroom, or even at home.) Teachers shout at him or accuse him of misbehaving, parents easily lose their patience, and the child can get quite angry at being told off for something he can't control. (Since what looks like high energy in a child could in fact be a case of extreme anxiety, or of hyperactivity, you might want to check with your pediatrician.)

Children who are very impulsive can experience similar problems. Adults tend to see them as unruly or disobedient, and they're often punished even though they're not trying to cause trouble. The child who is a little more impulsive, or more active, than most children is still normal; but life can be harder for him.

Children who are often ill are also faced with additional stress. Not only might they be anxious about their health, but parents are anxious around them. Because they're in and out of school, they might feel left out of the gang, or at a loss academically, contributing to an already developing sense of themselves as fragile. Even a physically healthy child who's home with the flu for a week might behave in a regressed, clingy, or demanding way, so it's easy to imagine the impact of frequent illness on a child's stress levels.

The Child's World of Meaning

The child's personal world of meaning plays a huge role in how easily he progresses through life, with all its snags. This inner world through which the child is continually interpreting experience is shaped not only by his personal history and how he has perceived it, but also by the often confused beliefs he has formed about the world, and by the conflicts and issues that are preoccupying him at the time.

Children have immature logical systems: They tend to invest their experiences with meanings that are highly subjective and egocentric, and to connect unrelated things into cause and effect

("Mom and Dad are fighting because I was bad yesterday"). Even on a daily level, if a parent is upset, the child thinks it must have something to do with him.

A child who's afraid to grow up may believe that in doing so he'll lose the love and protection of his parents; his belief might be based on a distorted interpretation, but nevertheless a certain, young child's way of thinking has led him to that conclusion. These kinds of stressful beliefs are just a part of growing up. Although they might throw the child for a period of time, he'll probably work it out for himself as he learns more about the world or if you can help him to pinpoint the confusion.

Normal Reactions to Stress

Here are some of the ways in which children might react to normal stress in their lives—whether the stress has to do with growing up or with external events. These reactions are not reasons to worry, but they might be signs for you to look at the kinds of things your child is being asked to cope with in his life, and may serve as indications that he needs a little extra attention, some soothing moments in his days, or a lessening in your expectations of him.

Regression. Regression is a normal part of development. All children regress from time to time, reverting to forms of behavior that they have for the most part given up. These more babylike behaviors, such as thumb sucking or baby talk, are your child's way of comforting himself in stressful times by returning to ways of acting that he associates with a more protected time in his life; when he's upset, it can be hard for him to mobilize the more grown-up parts of his personality. A classic example is the child who, after a sibling is born, temporarily abandons his toilet training or reverts to the bottle. Although he's a big brother now, he's not ready to feel like one yet.

Regressive pulls—not wanting to venture out into the

world—happen at all ages. A six- or seven-year-old who's had a demanding day at school may need extra attention at bedtime, or seem less interested in going out to play with a friend than in staying home with his parents. Many children today live lives that are far busier and more sophisticated than the lives their parents knew as children. As a result, you might find yourself surprised to hear your six-year-old computer wiz suddenly revert to baby talk, or your eight-year-old suddenly plead helplessness when you ask her to tie her laces. Don't worry if this happens now and again: She just needs to recharge.

Expressions of Stress—Tics, Nightmares, and Fears. You might worry about nervous tics, nightmares, nail biting, and thumb sucking, because you know that these behaviors are a reflection of internal stress. However, these nervous habits and reactions do appear from time to time as children face the challenges of growing up and dealing with day-to-day life.

As I've said, many children today are asked to grow up very fast, and do so in a very busy world. In single-parent and dual-career families particularly, there might not be a great deal of time to attend to a child's neediness. Stress resulting from the daily wear and tear of children's heavily scheduled lives may therefore emerge in the form of symptoms of stress of one sort or another, such as irritability, sleep problems, difficulty concentrating, restlessness, fearfulness, tics, or nightmares. These behaviors are very common and generally temporary—a tic might come and go for a couple of months; he might have nightmares every night for a few weeks. Unless the symptoms are very severe, or unusually prolonged, there's no need to take action. But like all symptoms of stress, they may be a sign for you to look more closely at your child's life, and at the kind of things he has to deal with.

Fears can be an indication that something—possibly something unrelated to the fear—is bothering the child. Feeling naughty lately, and anticipating the wrath of an angry parent, a young child can feel very vulnerable in a dark room where angry monsters are surely lurking.

Most parents know that certain ages bring typical fears, particularly in the threes to fives, when children can think "What if . . ." but don't have the kind of experience of the world that would reassure them that these "ifs" rarely happen. Your young child might develop a fear of being sucked down the bathtub drain; of getting lost while out shopping with Mom; of monsters under the bed; of injury to the self. These are normal and transitory fears. There's no need to force your child to overcome them; he will anyway, in time.

Sometimes fears are related to scary incidents that a child can't forget; it might even be generalized, so that the fear that started with one angry dog gets transferred to all dogs, and the fear of dogs then spreads to all furry creatures. But the origin is something real. Only when fears seem to be overwhelming your child or seriously interfering with his life need you think about consulting a professional. Later in this chapter, where I talk about specific symptoms, I'll discuss the difference between normal fears and phobias.

A CRY FOR HELP? KNOWING THE SIGNS

With all these normal snags and reactions occurring at different times throughout your child's life, it can be very difficult to know if a problem requires professional evaluation or if you can safely wait for it to go away by itself. If, after all of your efforts to put things right you're still concerned, you can ask yourself the following questions.

Is My Child Experiencing Prolonged and Intense Discomfort?

When a therapist speaks in terms of a child's discomfort, she means that he is stuck in some way of behaving or feeling that he doesn't like, or that's causing him pain. There's some negative reaction going on that is causing the child to be very upset in one way or another, whether the upset is expressed in disruptive or aggressive behavior, in trouble with a developmental task such as toilet training, in deep-seated fears such as the fear of separation, or through an overwhelming state of anxious confusion, sadness, or anger. I should point out here that occasionally a child can be showing symptoms of an emotional problem without actually experiencing any discomfort. For instance, he might seem content to withdraw self-protectively into his room and turn down all play dates. In other words, discomfort is not the only way of measuring a child's mental health.

Sometimes symptoms occur that you feel might be related to a particular event at home (maybe a divorce, or a new baby in the family) even though they occur in a seemingly unrelated area, like school. Don't expect your child to tell you what's upsetting him; he often doesn't even know himself. The opposite can also be true. I recently had a visit from a former patient, whose mother reported her to be looking unhappy, fighting with her father for the first time, and being oppositional at home. The girl's parents thought she must be upset about something that was going on in the family, but they couldn't think what. Their daughter, however, told me that the only problem area in her life was school, where her best friend kept dumping her for another friend, and she always felt so left out.

At other times symptoms have a completely mysterious origin, and parents are totally baffled by a child's behavior. Mark's parents began to consult me when he was three about his violent tantrums, his bullying, his resistance to anything he was asked to do. If he said his name was Joe, Joe it had to be. If he wanted pasta for dinner and was given eggs, he'd fly into a rage. He would say, "I didn't go to school today," when it was clear that he had. "I didn't, no I didn't. Say I didn't go to school today!" and everyone would have to agree.

This went on every day for months, and yet nothing apparent was happening in his life that could explain his behavior.

His parents were not only exhausted and miserable, they were baffled. They knew that Mark didn't really enjoy making life impossible for them—but then why was he doing it? They had no way of seeing that he felt he had to act in a way that said, "I'm okay because I'm stronger than you are." He was stuck in a very uncomfortable feeling of not liking himself, and the most effective way he could find to feel better was by controlling everyone around him and thereby feeling strong.

Different children express their discomfort in different ways. Although there are certainly frequent exceptions, many boys tend to act out their feelings in out-of-control ways such as naughty behavior, whereas girls are often quietly sad or withdrawn. Even anger can express itself in very reserved ways. Naturally, the loudest signals generally get the quickest response from parents, but the fact is that the quiet child can easily be in as much pain. Some parents once brought their feisty, tantrum-prone son to me for treatment, but were not as concerned about his sister, who lay terrified in a fetal position on the floor every time she was upset.

As I mentioned earlier, parents can be very confused by children who are doing fine at home but are reported by teachers to be disruptive in the classroom—it's easy to decide that the teacher is at fault. Every once in a while a child does come up against an insensitive teacher. But my own experience is that an insensitive teacher is seldom the sole cause of a child's troubles—after all, not every child in the class is reacting in such a powerful way. I feel that parents need to ask themselves, why is my child failing to adapt as others are, and what might happen in the future as he faces other less-than-ideal situations?

How Long Has the Problem Been Going On, and How Intense Is it?

Of course, a certain amount of discomfort is only to be expected in certain circumstances. But if it's entirely out of proportion, or if it doesn't seem to subside despite all your care and the efforts of the school, then there may be a problem.

You have to use your own judgment in deciding how long is too long, and how intense seems appropriate or reasonable. Basically, it all depends on the situation. For instance, if somebody close to a child dies, it can take a long time for him to get over it—don't expect the problem to go away too soon. What you should look for is some lessening of symptoms as months go by.

Similarly, a child who feels terrible all afternoon because another child slighted him at recess is showing a normal if overblown response to a common situation. But if two days later the injury is still echoing, and he can't seem to forgive the perpetrator or he resists going back to the playground because he's determined to avoid the scene of the crime, and if this happens repeatedly when the child is slighted, then your child is experiencing a lot of excess pain.

The same can be said for problems that seemed initially to be age-related. It's natural for a child of two to be oppositional. But if that child is still screaming "no" to your every "yes" at the age of four, then she may need help in moving forward. I'll talk about individual problems and the ages at which they can be expected later in this chapter.

Is My Child's Problem Affecting Other Areas of His Development?

Many emotional symptoms in childhood can adversely affect a child's development in one or more areas. Mark, for instance (the three-year-old who was bullying his family as a way of feeling stronger), felt so bad about himself in general that he couldn't take the important step of giving up his diaper; soon he would be turning four and starting nursery school, but the school was reluctant to accept him until he learned to use the toilet. I worked both with Mark and with his parents, and by the time school started, we had made enough progress in therapy so that he was able to overcome his resistance to the potty, although there was still plenty of work to be done around the overriding issue—Mark's sense of himself.

Children's emotional problems can hinder their development in other, more obvious ways. The child who, preoccupied with worries, cannot concentrate in school is being intellectually deprived; if she can't eat or sleep over a significant period of time, she may be deprived of good health; children who bite or hit at an age when their peers have ceased to do so get excluded by peers, and are bound to be held up in the development of social skills, as is the child who can't play because she's clinging constantly to her mother. And if her life is constricted by fears or phobias, she can't explore the wealth of new experiences the world has to offer her.

In my view, children need, more than anything else, opportunities to experience themselves as competent and effective if they are to develop healthy self-esteems, something I can't emphasize enough. Anything that hinders a child from mastering problems in his life, or from learning new skills, interferes with that important area of development. For this reason and others, you should seek professional evaluation if your child's difficulties are affecting his day-to-day life in any ongoing way that you feel might be hindering his social, physical, or intellectual development.

Is My Child's Problem Spreading to Other Areas?

Children tend to have symptoms in vulnerable areas. A child who has never been a good sleeper is most likely to develop a sleep-related disorder when he's emotionally weakened. A child who has never been good at separating from his parents will go tentatively into the world when things are going well in his life, but will cling desperately to Mom and Dad when his emotional strength is depleted by extra stress.

And yet sometimes symptoms get added on, so that discomfort spreads and worsens. A child may start by wetting the bed, then after a few weeks develop sleep problems, and the next thing you know he's screaming when you try and leave him at nursery school. Mark, the boy whose problems initially expressed themselves in his need to control things, started waking up crying in the mornings and saying how he hated himself. Initially it had seemed as if he might resolve his troubles by himself, but at this point it became clear that Mark was in need of help. Not only had his controlling behavior (his solution to feeling weak) been going on for more than six months, growing more intense as time went on, but it had backfired and was now making him feel terrible about himself. When symptoms snowball in this way, take it as a sign that your child might need some help from a professional.

Is the Family Affected by the Child's Problem?

Sometimes a child's problem has an adverse effect on the whole family. Parents are constantly exhausted by day-to-day outbursts and demands, while siblings feel deprived of attention because the child has made himself the focus of virtually every family moment. One child, David (whom we'll meet again later in the book), needed so much attention from his parents that his younger brother felt quite neglected, and on top of that the brother became the victim of unrelenting hostility from this deeply unhappy child.

Parents often disagree about how the child with a problem should be handled. As in Stephanie's case, perhaps one parent believes that more discipline is necessary, while the other feels that greater indulgence will help. They might even blame each other for what's happening. The conflict that results from these kinds of disagreements can strain a marriage, and in the process all children suffer as they become the object of parental battles. Moreover, when parents don't support each other in setting limits, the child receives very confusing, mixed messages. The authority of the firmer parent is undermined, and the child can always use the more lenient parent as an excuse for ignoring limits. Children need limits that are consistently set by both parents.

Although a child's difficulties can become a source of tension between parents, they can at least have a sense of being in it together, and they can provide each other occasional relief from the strain. A single parent, on the other hand, has nobody to share the burdens with, and can feel completely alone with and overwhelmed by the child's problems. Also, the child's problems can become part of the ongoing fight between two separated parents.

TYPICAL CHILDHOOD PROBLEMS

As these guidelines show, you have to look at specific problems in their context before you can really get a sense of what they imply about the child's emotional health: He doesn't listen; he can't sit still; he fights with other children; he won't go to sleep at night; he won't let go of my skirt; he seems to be trying to make me mad; he's started wetting his bed. In themselves, these annoying or worrisome behaviors don't necessarily mean that your child needs help. They're usually short-lived and not very intense. As I pointed out earlier in this chapter, there are all sorts of internal and external stresses in children's lives that can explain their occasional stumblings, and one isolated problem rarely indicates treatment.

If these kinds of behavior persist, though, you may want to

consult with a professional. Let's look individually at the kinds of problems that parents worry about most.

Oppositional Behavior

"He'll never do what he's told." "He's impossible to deal with." Is this just a stage the child is going through, or is it a sign that he's having trouble in some area of his life?

I would say that for a short period of time—say, up to six months or so—and at a certain age, this kind of behavior can be quite normal. As I've already described, children of two are inclined to say no to their parents as a way of expressing their autonomy. An older child, too, might go through an oppositional stage in response to the birth of a sibling, or because something is going on outside of the home that's troubling her—perhaps she's being picked on in school, or she's anxious about an upcoming exam. But even the most pervasive "no's" can go away by themselves after a short time.

Some children will fight their parents around one or two specific things—perhaps around schoolwork, because it makes them nervous—but when it comes to tidying their room or running out to the store with you, they'll go along quite easily. You might want to give a child like this some extra help with his studies, but there's certainly no need to rush off to a therapist. It's only when a child feels he has to fight his parents around everything, and when that fighting goes on for an extended period of time and seems to have a fixed quality, that I would advise talking to a professional.

In such a situation, you might say, "He's always been like this; it's just his personality"—but there's a problem there nevertheless. Whether his oppositionalism stems from fears (as did Stephanie's), or because he feels betrayed and angry about something, or is more central to his temperament, this child needs some help learning to deal with the demands of the real world. Otherwise, in his need to oppose, he might cut himself off from all sorts of experiences that are important to his development. Also, whatever the reason for his oppositionalism, at some point the angry responses provoked by such a child can make him feel like an awful person, and then he might need help not only in relating to people in a different way, but also in feeling differently about himself.

Aggressive Behavior

To some extent, aggressive behavior is a normal part of human interaction. Some people are naturally more aggressive than others, as are some ages. Most parents know that two-year-olds tend to bite, hit, pull hair, and scream the moment another child takes a toy from them or frustrates them in their play; this is quite age-appropriate. But three-year-olds should be learning to control these antisocial impulses, and to use language instead as a way of dealing with life's frustrations.

By the time a child is entering kindergarten, he should be showing that he's able to control a majority of his physically aggressive reactions, if not all of them. The more a child is able to use words to express anger, the less likely he is to do it through physical means. Of course, it's very important that you as a parent are also using words rather than physical means in your dealings with your child, since he models his behavior on yours.

Continued and constant aggression may be a sign that a child has not learned to channel his feelings in more acceptable ways. If your child responds aggressively to frustrations that most other children seem to be able to take in their stride, it may mean that he has a very low tolerance for frustration. If your child's level of aggression doesn't seem to be on the wane, despite your attempts to help him find other means of responding; if he is still hitting other children, and especially if other people are getting hurt or if the child's relationships with others are being affected by his behavior, then you should probably seek a professional evaluation.

Sometimes there are real emotional issues fueling a child's aggression. A child might seek to bolster his very low self-esteem by bossing everyone around. Others are reported as being very aggressive in school, yet you see no signs of aggression at home; very often these children claim that they're being picked on. A child who feels unhappy in his home life, or who has very low self-esteem, can go to school and take out his unhappiness on other children; the slightest, most trivial thing can provoke him. If your child's teacher tells you that his behavior is disrupting the classroom, it's best not to dismiss the information as wrong just because he's quiet at home. As I've said, something may be going on in his life that requires attention.

On the other hand, bouts of increased aggression can result from the kinds of stress that children suffer from time to time, when something upsetting is going on in their lives such as a divorce or the birth of a sibling. If your child suddenly starts acting aggressively at home or in school, and you're aware of an external reason for his outbursts, this may be a sign for you to help him cope better with the stresses in his life; hopefully, the behavior will pass.

Temper Tantrums

Parents often worry about children's temper tantrums. Should they still be having them? Are they just trying to get attention? Of course, two- and even three-year-olds are famous for tantrums, but if a toddler is screaming most of the day, you'll probably want to check it out with a professional—if for no other reason than to find out if you could be handling the tantrums more effectively. During a child's nursery-school years, you should start to see him beginning to cope with frustration, anger, or sadness in different and more acceptable ways than by throwing tantrums. By the time a child enters elementary school, he certainly should have developed a fairly good level of control, and ought to be using words to express himself rather than tantrums. For a while, though, he might still have the occassional outburst.

There are a number of possible causes for an older child's repeated tantrums. If, by the age of five or six, you see no sign of them subsiding, or if they're still a regular part of his day-to-day life, or he can't be consoled and helped out of a tantrum, then the child certainly needs help in finding other ways of expressing his feelings, and some deeper issues may also need to be addressed—why is he feeling this way? Also, if an older child suddenly starts having temper tantrums, this too might be a signal that something is wrong. In both cases, it would be wise to discuss this with a professional.

Shyness or Withdrawal

It's important to understand the difference between shyness—initial discomfort with new acquaintances—and withdrawal—the moving away in an ongoing pattern from meaningful connections. Shyness is simply part of a child's innate temperament, whereas withdrawal can be a sign that something is amiss.

Susan's parents, for instance, were very worried about her daughter's shyness. Every time they were around strangers Susan would be very frightened, and would want to go home. Her parents' concern was that Susan might have some trouble in her social development. But as soon as Susan walked into my office for the first time, I could see that, although she was very shy, she was also very interested in getting to know me. She kept watching me whenever she thought I wasn't looking, and when I caught her eye, she'd smile and quickly look away. Obviously she wasn't a child who would shut people out; if someone gave her time, she would find a way of making contact because she liked people. Susan didn't need help, although I did feel that she could benefit from being shown a few ways of coping with her anxiety around strangers. I also worked with her parents to help them tune in to her signals—signals that showed when she needed help, and when she was actually coping quite well, even though she wouldn't admit it.

The withdrawn child, on the other hand, is not interested in getting to know strangers. No matter how much time he's given, he can't or doesn't want to warm up to anyone in any but the most superficial sense, because there is something too painful or simply not compelling about the world of people, or about relationships. He turns inward into his own world—"Just leave me alone; I'm not interested in playing with anyone; I don't want to see any other kids." When a child withdraws as a defense against anxiety (perhaps he's too convinced people won't like him or treat him well), treatment could help alleviate the underlying anxiety.

Other children, however, may always prefer quiet, solitary play or play with just a few select friends, and they may comfortably continue to live their lives in this way, becoming more interested in the world of ideas than of people as they grow up, or forming fewer but not any less fulfilling relationships.

Depression

Depression was once thought of as a condition of adulthood, but in recent years it has become apparent that children, and even infants, can be depressed. If your child seems uncharacteristically sad and listless, is having sleep or eating problems, is unable to concentrate in school, or suffers from repeated psychosomatic illnesses, then you will probably want to look into the causes. Even acting out can be a sign—people of all ages have a tendency to mask their depression through other behaviors that look more angry than sad. Of course, if there seems to be an external source of the child's depression—something going on in his life that you would expect him to be sad about—then his feelings may be quite reasonable and should subside as the child comes to terms with things.

Talk of Suicide. Sometimes a child who is depressed will talk about killing himself; one four-year-old was referred to me because she was threatening to jump off the roof. If your child talks often about killing herself or wanting to be dead—even if you don't take the talk seriously—this should be examined by a professional, if for no other reason than to get a measure of the child's despair.

Psychosomatic Symptoms

Some physical disorders are exacerbated or even caused by stress or upset. These include emotionally based stomachaches or headaches, bronchial asthma, irritable bowel syndrome. If you feel that your child's bodily complaints are related to anxiety or tension, you should talk to someone about it.

Phobias and Fears

As I've said, fears are a normal part of growing up. Many things are frightening to children. Young children of two and three are particularly prone to fears—of loud noises, separation, monsters, to name a few. In my experience, fears are likely to pass quickly in young children if parents help to soothe and reassure them, although in the case of a very fearful child you might like to see someone and get some suggestions on how to encourage him to become less anxious about the world, or to cope more constructively with his anxieties.

Phobias, on the other hand, seriously interfere in some way with the child's everyday life, shutting off a part of his world. Not only does he feel the need to avoid the things that scare him, but his fears spread by association. He may be unable, for instance, to look at a book that might have a picture of a lion, because he's terrified of lions, or to go to a birthday party, because he's scared of balloons. One of the most common phobias in childhood is the one that stops the child from going around his own home; he might even be unable to stay in his own room alone. Underlying this kind of phobia is usually some kind of separation problem.

Unlike fears, phobias cannot be soothed away by a parent checking under the bed for monsters, or promising to be back by four. The child himself might even know that there's really no rational basis for his terror of dogs, or of water, but he also knows that he just can't help it. As one little girl told me, "I know it can't happen, but I can't stop myself from thinking about it."

In my experience, there is often a powerful anger underlying a phobia. Children who are "school-phobic," for instance, are not only anxious over separation, they're furious that they've been left, or "dumped." The phobia might seem completely unrelated to the source of the child's anger. One girl, angry over her parents' divorce, could not stay in her room alone. Phobias, by definition, are long-lasting and intense. So even though your child's phobia might eventually pass by itself, you would probably want to seek help if it interferes with his life on a regular basis.

School Phobia. School phobia is one of the most common phobias of childhood, yet one that clearly has to be attended to, as it interferes with an essential part of your child's life. It's also important to understand why your child differs from the majority of children, whose natural anxieties about being in nursery school or kindergarten don't interfere with their ability to be there and benefit.

How can you tell the difference between the child who's school-phobic, and the child who simply doesn't want to be left in school because he doesn't like it? There are certain behaviors that a parent can look for, although the differences are not always so clear-cut. The child who is really phobic of school cannot tolerate being left there for any length of time. He'll scream and yell until his parent comes back, and he'll also spend his evenings worrying about the dreadful morning to come. On the other hand, the child who is merely uncomfortable about school or would prefer to be home might cry stormily for a time, but will soon show signs of settling down to enjoy himself.

Separation Anxiety

Although most children react to separation from their parents, for many it's never a problem. From the youngest age they're happy to go to strangers, and comfortable when their parents leave the room. Other children develop a tendency early on to fear separation from their parents and continue to become somewhat upset by even brief separations for several years. Both are quite normal.

A child's clinginess can sometimes be the result of something that's happening at home—perhaps there's a new baby in the family, or a new caretaker. In this kind of situation, the separation problem should pass in time. But if your child suddenly grows clingy and you can see no reason for it, or if he never managed to grow out of his early fear of separation, then you might like to seek a professional's advice. When a school-age child finds it difficult to say good-bye and go to school, or to play with friends in the park while you sit nearby, this kind of dependency can really interfere with his day-to-day life and social development, besides making him feel miserable.

There are several ways in which a therapist can help make the bonds between a child and his parents more flexible, and increase the child's confidence in his own ability to be apart from his parents for limited periods of time. One of the things I do to help a child in this area is to shore up the relationship with the father, as a step away from the mother. Then I try to gradually and safely facilitate relationships with other adults in the child's life—a teacher, for instance. At the same time, it's important to develop the child's sense of herself as capable and able to handle things more independently.

Anxious Behavior

Some children grow overly anxious in a most general way. They might seem generally unhappy, preoccupied with worries, and very dependent on constant reassurance from parents that they won't be left by themselves, that nothing bad is going to happen, and so on. However much you reassure these children, the worries return. Naturally, this kind of anxiety can easily interfere with the child's ability to concentrate in school or venture out into new experiences.

Anxious children don't have a sense of their own ability to master things, and so they tend to avoid situations that worry them rather than try and cope with them. If you can help the child to master these things rather than to avoid them, the anxieties will lessen as he learns that he is capable (though sometimes with help) of making things right. However, if the worries continue or grow stronger, and the child's life is being interfered with, at home or in school, then you should seek professional evaluation.

Obsessive-Compulsive Behavior

Many children are compulsive by nature, becoming caught up in rituals that have a magical flavor—for instance, not walking on the cracks in the sidewalk. Young children especially tend to be ritual bound, insisting rigidly on a certain story before bed each night, or on a special bear to hug. These kinds of bedtime rituals can be hard to give up.

However, should a child continue with these kinds of rituals after the age of six, either taking them to an extreme, panicking if they're interfered with, or allowing them to spread into many areas of life, this can mean that the child is trying to quell some powerful anxieties magically. If a large part of your child's life seems to be caught up in compulsive behavior, and he has to spend a lot of time making his world safe through arbitrary rituals, he might be in need of some help.

Nail Biting, Thumb Sucking, Tics, Etc.

See "Expressions of Stress," page 17.

Antisocial Behavior

All children at some time lie, steal, or engage in other forms of antisocial behavior. As they grow older and are capable of learning to control their impulses and to understand society's rules and take the other person's perspective, then these behaviors should become more of a cause for concern.

Lying. All small children lie, in part because they don't fully understand the distinction between truth and fantasy, or a little later because they see lying simply as a convenient way of staying out of trouble. Lying is something that can be worked on in the family; parents can communicate family values to the child, and can send firm messages of approval or disapproval in response to truthful or untruthful reporting.

However, if a child is past seven and still lies a great deal of the time, then he may be having a problem controlling his impulses; every time he does something "bad," he is terrified of the consequences and lies to cover up. Also, if he seems to consistently indulge in total fabrications rather than merely exaggeration (all children brag and boast), in order to impress friends with pretended achievements or possessions, then he might be feeling a strong need to bolster his self-esteem. In either case, you should consider seeking professional evaluation.

Lying and Fantasy. Some children seem to live in a fantasy world of their own, inventing and telling fantastic, detailed stories about themselves and their lives that are completely untrue. Usually, the child feels that he needs these fantasies because he is unhappy about who he really is, or what he really has. He may feel deprived or uninteresting. Obviously, a child who has to reject an accurate picture of himself or his life could benefit from some help in self-acceptance and in constructively rechanneling energies.

Stealing. Stealing, like lying, is quite common and normal among very young children. Until the age of about four, a child cannot differentiate clearly between what's his and what belongs to others. If he leaves the park with another child's pail, it's because he liked it, wanted it, and saw no reason why he couldn't have it. By the age of five or six, most children know the difference between what's theirs and someone else's, but they might still steal once in a while because they can't control the powerful urge to have what they see and want.

Again, parents can help children to learn that stealing is not allowed. If, every time your child takes something that doesn't belong to him, you immediately remind him that stealing is wrong, that it makes the other person feel bad, that you don't approve of it, and that there are consequences to stealing (the child has to give the stolen object back), then the behavior should soon cease. Although it might not be a sign of anything serious, if chronic stealing persists at any age past five (despite your efforts to help the child stop), you may want to consult with a professional in order to understand the problem better.

Eating and Sleep Problems

With both eating and sleep problems, it's always worth checking with your pediatrician to see if he's concerned before you think about consulting a therapist.

Eating. "He'll only eat pasta and hot dogs." Parents, concerned about proper nutrition, naturally worry when their children refuse all but a few choices of food. But in fact a restricted diet is not something you should worry about. As long as the child is eating enough to sustain him, there is little point in battling three times a day over meals for the time being.

You should, however, ask yourself whether your child's constricted eating patterns are part of a larger picture. Is he having trouble trying new things and adjusting to the demands of life—an important part of the process of growing up? Is this a wonderful way for him to fight back and maintain control, because he knows how badly you want him to eat different foods? Or is the child simply a finicky eater, in which case he will probably become more flexible with age?

Sudden Changes in Eating Patterns. If your child was a good eater and suddenly stops eating, or always ate regular meals and is suddenly filling himself up at every opportunity, this might be reflecting something that's going on in his life. It might be some temporary event you can pinpoint, such as beginning school. But if it goes on for a long time, or if you can't understand it, you might want to discuss it with a professional.

Pica. Pica is the name for a disorder in which there's a need to eat nonfood items, such as chalk or paint, for instance. It is seen as a potential health problem in childhood because children don't know what's dangerous to eat. Of course, all babies put things in their mouths, but when a child is three or four and his parents are no longer watching him so closely, pica should be given the attention of a professional.

Sleep Problems. Sleeping patterns, like eating patterns, can reflect something that's going on in a child's life. Some children can't go to bed or fall asleep because they're afraid of separation. Others become so preoccupied with their lives that they lie awake, running the day through their head; one little boy used to bring his schoolbooks to bed because he was so worried about how well he was going to do in class the next day. On the other hand, a child who doesn't seem to be sleeping enough might simply be the kind of person who doesn't need much sleep.

A child who can't stay in bed through the night, but wakes regularly and needs your help to go back to sleep, might need help learning that he can fall asleep by himself.

Nightmares and Night Terrors. If your child suffers from extended and unusually painful episodes of nightmares or night terrors, you will probably want to look into the reasons with a professional.

Bed-Wetting (Enuresis)

Because it can be explained by either biological or emotional factors or both, bed-wetting is a very complicated issue. Let me start by saying that until the age of six, bed-wetting is not normally considered a problem. After this age, bed-wetting is still occasionally seen as a physiological rather than an emotional problem; perhaps the child has not yet achieved muscular control over his bladder. It's certainly advisable to mention the problem to the child's pediatrician, who can rule out any medical causes, but if the bed-wetting is part of a larger picture of emotional anxiety, then you should probably consult a therapist.

Although bed-wetting may not mean a problem in itself, it can *cause* problems. It's not just a question of social embarrassments for the child—sleepovers with a friend, for instance, can be quite difficult—but also of how the child feels about himself. Constant bed-wetting can be a humiliating and demeaning experience for a child. You might well want to seek a professional evaluation on how to help him with these feelings if he seems

very upset about the problem or if you feel that it is part of a
larger picture of difficulties.

Soiling (Encopresis)

Encopresis is far less common than enuresis, but nevertheless it
is a fairly widespread condition. Although there might be medical causes that should be ruled out by the child's pediatrician,
encopresis is often the result of the child withholding bowel
movements until they harden, at which point liquid feces leak
from around the blockage. As he withholds, he might suffer some
abdominal pain. So, what could look for a few days like diarrhea
turns out to be a chronic case of constipation. Although the child
might simply feel uncomfortable about using the bathroom in his
new school, or fearing pain after a previous, painful bowel
movement, if the soiling continues, it might be a sign of some
deeper issues that need looking into.

Regular soiling, even more than wetting, is an extremely
damaging experience for any child of pre-school age or older.
Not only does it create a high level of self-disgust in the child, but
other people—children and adults—easily become disgusted,
and the child's self-image can suffer dramatically. Besides the
fact that the child may need help with these consequences of
encopresis, if the problem is not medical, you should seek help
from a therapist who can work with you both in finding and
resolving the problems that are causing it.

Masturbation

It's certainly not unusual for small children to handle their
genitals, especially in times of stress or boredom. But very few
children grow up without learning from someone that masturbation is not acceptable as a public act, and most children quickly
learn to keep it for more private moments. By the time children
enter school, they should be demonstrating some control over

this area, and developing a sense of private versus public acts—although masturbation at nap time is fairly common. If a child of around six doesn't have the social sense or the internal controls to stop playing with his genitals while he's in the company of others (in spite of appropriate parental guidance), then he may have a problem deserving of a professional's attention. Sometimes a child's preoccupation with his genitals is his way of comforting himself in times of anxiety.

CHILDREN TO WATCH

Every child has his own threshold beyond which things become intolerable; one child can take certain stresses in his stride, while another has a problem with it. Just because your neighbor's child suffered excessively when her parents divorced doesn't mean that yours will.

How easily a child manages in times of stress depends on many factors: his temperament, his vulnerable areas (a mother's return to work would be most stressful for a child with unresolved separation problems), and what else is going on in his life at the time. Some children can tolerate a great deal when things are going well and they feel strong about themselves. But when their sense of equilibrium is weakened by things that are happening in their inner or outer worlds, they can't cope.

Many factors can make children at higher risk of needing help, among them divorce, learning disabilities, physical handicap, parents dependent on drugs or alcohol, and certain traumatic events, such as sexual abuse or the death of someone close. Children who are faced with these special stresses in their lives should be watched. There may be nothing innately fragile about any of these children, but what they're being asked to deal with in their daily lives might be more than any child can tolerate smoothly. Because they have more to handle than other children, they may need something extra from their parents in the way of attention and listening, and ultimately they may need help.

Before we look at the most common "risk" factors, I should point out that it can be helpful for parents whose children are at risk in the ways I just outlined to arrange for a one-time consultation with a therapist. I often see parents who are concerned because they are just about to announce a divorce to their children, or a new baby is about to be born. I'll give them suggestions on how they can best introduce this new information to their child, and what to look out for in the way of related symptoms. Parents have also consulted me for advice and reassurance about how to help a child who has been exposed to some tragic or very upsetting event. (I'll deal further with this kind of preventative measure in the next chapter.)

The Silent Cry—When a Child Hides His Grief. While some children respond in highly visible ways to tragedies or crises in their lives, once in a while a child will show no obvious signs of the grief they are experiencing. One little boy, Robby, is a good example—his troubles revolved around the death of someone whom he adored, but the child who has experienced any kind of trauma can respond in the same way.

When Robby was six, his father died suddenly and completely unexpectedly. One year later Robby's mother brought him in to see me. Since his father's death, Robby had shown no signs of grief; he just said, "It's okay, I've got plenty of friends, I don't miss him." That was all; he had never talked about his father, about his death, or about his own feelings. But Robby did have symptoms that concerned his mother. He couldn't concentrate in school, he couldn't sit still, he didn't listen to the teacher.

When a child quietly goes on with her life after a traumatic event, and shows very few reactions, she might be dealing with the situation quietly and at times finding relief by putting things out of her mind, as children can do so well. A child doesn't have to have a big grieving period for you to know she's coping. But when there's a total absence of feelings expressed and yet you're seeing symptoms, then you know that the child is paying a price. She needs help in talking about it, and in dealing with feelings that are too painful for her to accept.

Children of Divorce

Divorce has become a fact of life for many children nowadays, whether as a reality or a nagging threat. Even if a child hasn't experienced divorce in his family, he might have a friend whose parents have separated, and may anxiously jump to conclusions when he sees his own parents arguing.

And yet while divorce is a powerful blow to any child, and leaves its mark in many indelible ways, quite a number of children are ultimately able to adapt and go on with their lives. You needn't automatically assume that just because your child is upset, he's going to need therapy. Far from it. It's quite natural for children to react in various ways to an event that is, after all, going to change their lives.

When parents divorce, stress occurs on many levels. First, there's the inevitable separation from one parent, even if it's just during weekdays or weekends. Then, there may be a move to a new house and a new school, or the start of day care so that Mom can take a job. One boy told me he was worried that he and his mother would become homeless, because it was his father who earned the money. He was also troubled by the thought that his mother might have to take a full-time job and wouldn't be there to care for him anymore.

Newly divorced parents are often upset, tense, lonely— emotions that a young child recognizes, but can't fully understand. Confused and anxious, he might even believe that he's the cause of this terrible thing that has happened. The child of divorce faces constant disappointment because he keeps hoping, for many years (even after one parent has remarried), that his mother and father will get back together again. Messy divorces involving custody battles or struggles over possessions can be especially stressful; in my experience, this kind of situation is more than many children can cope with in the absence of extra supports, especially if anything else stressful should come along.

Warning Signs. When should a child's reactions be seen as a sign that help is needed? The same rules that apply in any other situation apply here: How long has the symptom gone on without lessening? Is it seriously affecting other areas of the child's life? Is it snowballing? Is it causing pain to other family members?

Even when parents are hovering close to the point of divorce but no separation has been mentioned, children might start to get panicky about the fights or obvious tensions that they're seeing. These days, children hardly need to be told about divorce—they can see it coming (occasionally even when it's not).

Six-year-old Kevin, for instance, felt that he had to be the one to stave off the possibility of his parents divorcing by becoming the peacemaker between them. He'd put his hands over his ears and yell for them to stop fighting. He'd even sacrifice himself for the sake of parental harmony. Kevin's is not an uncommon story of the kind of strain that the mere threat of divorce can put on a child. One day, Kevin was all set to go on a trip to the beach with his father and some friends, when his mother decided that the sun was too strong and he was liable to burn. His father argued that Kevin would be fine—he'd use sunscreen and keep his T-shirt on—but his mother had backed herself into a corner and insisted that no, Kevin could not go. The friends arrived with their own child, the argument continued, and finally, although Kevin had been looking forward to this day for weeks and everyone else was going, he suddenly changed his mind and said, "It's okay, I'll just stay home. I didn't want to go anyway." He may have even felt responsible for the fight, since it centered around his well-being.

When a child feels responsible for making peace between his parents, or is actively protecting whomever he thinks of as the weaker parent, you can take this as a warning sign that he is under a great deal of stress. Another warning sign comes when the child starts to align himself with either the mother or the father, as Kevin did when his parents' divorce began to seem inevitable. He started to tell his father, "I'll take care of you, Daddy. You can get divorced and I'll come and live with you and take care of you." He was choosing sides, becoming increasingly angry with his mother and setting the stage for a life with his father, in order to ensure his own future. When a child is really paying a price—feeling responsible or pushed into taking sides, for instance—then you might want to consult with someone who can give you some suggestions about how to make things easier for your child.

Sometimes the child who most needs help is the one whose problem ends up being ignored. Maybe your son's reaction to your divorce has been noisy, disruptive, tearful, while your daughter's has been quiet. Parents have to learn to listen to a variety of signals.

If you're still worried after some time has passed, it may help to consult a therapist about your child—but go quietly, and don't involve your child until you've received professional advice. After hearing the whole story, the therapist might tell you that it's too soon to expect your child's anger or sadness to subside.

Remarriage. A parent's remarriage brings its own stresses, especially to an only child who's grown used to the undivided attention that is, after all, one of the perks of divorce for some children. I won't forget the twelve-year-old girl who, in talking to me about her stepfather and half brother, expressed a common sentiment: "I just can't forget all those wonderful years . . . it was just my mother and me."

Remarriage can bring all sorts of additional stresses: There may be new siblings; there's a new parent who might sometimes care for the child, but who in the child's view has questionable rights to discipline ("You're not my mother! You can't tell me what to do!"); there could be conflicting loyalties and painful feelings of disloyalty to the child's real parent should he happen to grow very attached to his new one; there could be many problems heaped on the plate of this child.

Adopted Children

The adopted child, like the child whose parents divorce, isn't necessarily at risk of developing emotional problems. But something special has happened, and so you might want to watch his progress and give him a little extra attention at the critical point in his life when he is first told about the adoption, or when he first reaches the age when he can understand it. Even if he has known since he was two, there comes a point around the age of six or seven when the information becomes meaningful to him— when he has the capacity to see that he once belonged to someone else who gave him up. He might feel a sudden sense of loss, or of having been dumped.

There are several legitimate approaches to discussing adoption with a child; this kind of information is readily available to adoptive parents. The most important factor is that you should be accepting of your child's reactions—whatever they might be.

Children with Learning Disabilities

Although having a learning disability does not in itself indicate the need for treatment, I'm including learning-disabled children within the group of children to watch. As the story I'm about to tell illustrates, these children are at high risk of developing an impaired self-esteem. The one concrete measure a child has of himself is his performance in school—whether it's which reading group he's been assigned to, his latest test scores, or the grades on his report card. Academic functioning is his daily, full-time job, and everyone knows how bad it feels to be doing one's job poorly.

A child was once brought to me who, at the age of nine, had just been diagnosed as learning disabled. During all her years in school she had been struggling, not only with the work itself but also with teachers who accused her of being an uncooperative student. By the time she came to me, she too thought that she was dumb and worthless. She told me, "I just don't pay attention in school." And on top of that she felt frustrated and helpless.

When she was finally given the label "learning disabled," the whole family grew very anxious. Her father angrily rejected the idea, yet at the same time he did believe it and felt terrified of the implications. His daughter was also very frightened. Nobody in the family really understood the meaning of this label that the girl had been given. She needed help—first of all help in understanding what it means to be learning disabled (and how so many people, once they leave school, flourish despite their disability), but mainly, help in counteracting her view of herself as stupid and worthless.

Mastery of tasks in general is such an important part of self-esteem development, and the learning-disabled child has to struggle, often unsuccessfully, to master tasks that are a challenge to children under the best of circumstances. Too often, his failures—even if only in one or two specific areas, such as writing and math—make him feel worthless all around.

As I've said, most children with learning problems don't require treatment. Most manage to cope with them, with the active support of school and family. There are many ways in which you can help your child at home, mainly by pointing out to him that he's not dumb but has problems in some specific areas;

by having realistic expectations for him and showing him how he can meet them ("If you work hard with your tutor, you'll write well enough to keep up with your class"); and by reminding him of his compensating strengths ("Your writing will never be as good as your math, which is one of your talents"). A good tutor can help the child develop lagging skills, and can help him compensate by using the areas where his strengths lie. A child with a good visual memory, for instance, can be taught to use it in his approach to learning.

Sometimes, though, none of these efforts are enough to stop a child from developing a deflated sense of himself. If you feel that your child has been made overwhelmingly anxious either by the troubles he's having in school or by the label itself, or is hiding his disappointments in himself behind a "what's the use" attitude, he may benefit from the help of a professional who can explain in clear terms what it means to be learning disabled, and who can work with him around the self-esteem issue.

The Difficult Child

A large group of normal children are born with personality features that interfere with their development and with the smooth flow of day-to-day living, features that make parenting them very tricky and exhausting. In order to help you understand what I mean by the difficult child, I'm going to tell you about life with Jack.

Jack was born irritable. Although he had warm, caring parents who knew how to say no yet were also able to allow their son the freedom to explore, nothing felt right with him. Although he could be a very happy baby, at times he'd push his mother away, and he was always difficult to comfort. From the earliest age he didn't eat right—he never really enjoyed the bottle, and later was very picky about the foods he would eat (not much more than pasta). He slept poorly, waking his parents up all

night long. He didn't deal well with strangers, and because he
was very inflexible, he disliked changes intensely.

In fact, Jack was intense in everything. He reacted with
intense emotional outbursts to the slightest frustration, and once
he was in a mood, it was hard to shake him out of it. Very few
things happened easily in Jack's life as he developed, and yet
none of this could be fully explained by any emotional or physiological disorder. He was just difficult, although there were
external factors that contributed to his very upset state.

A difficult child is not necessarily a child who needs help.
But since I'm consulted so often about children who can simply
be described as difficult, let me explain why and how problems
can develop. Children who are "difficult" from birth need a
certain kind of parenting—a kind that doesn't always come
naturally. Sometimes it's a matter of "fit"; some parents can
intuitively understand what their difficult baby needs from
them, but if a difficult infant is paired with parents who are
made very anxious by his behavior, or whose personalities don't
lend themselves to calm, firm limit setting, then problems can
develop.

A difficult child's behavior in infancy—his unconsolable
fussiness and his constant demands on those close to him—can
make parents feel anxious, insecure in their parenting abilities,
and/or angry. Jack's mother, for instance, became so worried
about her son and experienced his upsets so powerfully that she
very quickly began to see and treat him as if he were terribly
fragile. When she first came to see me, she described her eight-
year-old as being terrified of people getting mad at him; he was
so used to being soothed by his very caring mother that he never
learned to tolerate any kind of disapproval from others, and he
never learned to master his fears by himself.

The difficult child's behavior is bound to affect the way that
people treat him. Parents and teachers easily lose their patience
with this kind of child. In turn, the child becomes angry and his

sense of himself as a bad or unlovable person can make him feel terrible. At this point his poor self-image, his inability to tolerate frustration, and his intensities all combine to make life stressful for him.

Parents who are already feeling overwhelmed by life—by the strain of juggling the demands of work and parenting, or by the difficulties of single parenting, for instance—can have an especially hard time finding the energy and patience needed to set firm, clear limits for a difficult child. After all, isn't it easier—when you're tired after a long day, and your little one's in a rage because you won't read him yet another story before bed, and you've already fought with him for ten minutes—to simply put off bedtime for a while longer? Wouldn't you rather avoid those tears that make you feel as if you've sorely wounded him, yet again?

If you are the parent of a difficult child, and your life seems like one long battle, you might want to consult someone who can help put things on the right track so your parenting meets your child's needs. In my experience, if parents can learn early to read the messages the child is sending, and can also learn how best to deal with the tricky situations that are an everyday part of living with and parenting the difficult child, then the problems can be resolved.

Pressured Children

Parents sometimes come to see me about their children and say, "I remember there was one day when she saw something really frightening—could that be what started this off?"

In fact, more than any single event in a child's life, it's the ongoing, repetitive quality of life that really shapes the way a child feels and can leave him feeling angry, anxious, or hurt. A life-style that's overly scheduled, and in which children are pressured to function on a level of performance that doesn't come naturally to them, can certainly take its toll.

It's very easy for children to feel that their parents just

don't have room in their lives for them. A child may decide that his parents don't really want him, or he might just feel shut out, hurried, or overwhelmed. In spite of all your efforts to provide the best for your child, he can easily experience a very hurried life-style as a signal that other things are more important to you than he and his needs are.

I once treated a little girl who felt exactly this way. She felt peripheral to her parents' lives. The pressures on her to be grown up were enormous, because there was no time in the life of the family for her to fuss and fight, dream and dawdle, as little children do. Since she was always being pushed forward and onward in her life, she struggled against every move she was required to make. This angry little girl was finally brought to me because of the constant, pitched battles she was having with her mother, which in part came out of her very rushed life-style.

Although there might not be much one can do about the realities of trying to balance work and parenting, these children might need a little extra emotional reassurance from their parents, and some flexibility wherever possible so that there's a little room for a child to be a child.

I hope that in the course of this chapter I've been able to give you a clearer sense of when and why you should talk to a professional about your child. One last point: You don't have to be certain about whether you're doing the right thing before you seek help, and you don't have to spend months anxiously wondering if it's a good idea. As I mentioned earlier, many therapists will see parents for a one-time consultation just to discuss worrying issues. I frequently do this; sometimes I recommend treatment, sometimes I give a few parenting suggestions in the hope that the problems can be resolved at home, and sometimes I only need to reassure parents that what seemed like an insurmountable problem is, in all likelihood, just a phase or a quirk of temperament. In the next chapter I'll discuss the consultation, and how you can best use it.

2

THE CONSULTATION:
FINDING A GOOD FIT

Y ou may remember Stephanie's parents, Mr. and Mrs. Baker, with whom I was speaking as we opened the first chapter of this book. They were sitting in my office, consulting with me about their troubled daughter and hoping that I might be the one who would be able to help her so that family life might return to normal. They told me that Stephanie cried every night and had nightmares; that she was easily angered and frustrated; that her self-esteem was low ("I can't do anything right"); that she didn't feel free to protect herself from other children; that she was shy, and new things were hard for her; and that she refused to do what she didn't want to do.

As the Bakers talked, I began to get a sense of this child who was making them so concerned, and who couldn't have been feeling very happy about herself either. And as I listened and responded to her parents, they began to form an opinion of me—whether they felt comfortable with me, and whether I was the right person to treat their child.

If Stephanie's problems had been very straightforward—a simple issue that didn't spread into other areas of her life, such as an isolated sleep problem—I might have been able to send her parents home after their first visit with some helpful advice, perhaps a more detailed plan of action for them to follow at home, and an invitation for them to call or visit if they needed some follow-up advice. Or I might have recommended that they see me a few times for parent-work sessions without ever having to bring their child into treatment. (I'll talk more about this form of treatment through parent contact in chapter 4, "Parent-Work.")

As it turned out, though, I felt from what Mr. and Mrs. Baker told me during our meeting that their daughter probably could benefit from some kind of therapy. She was obviously experiencing a lot of pain, and it was apparent to me that the symptoms did interfere with a large part of this small girl's life. Also, because I felt that her problems had to do with her over-dependency on her mother and her inability to separate, I thought that she needed some help that was separate from the help a mother can provide. So I asked to see Stephanie in order to find out more about her.

My meetings with Stephanie constituted the second phase of the consultation. I saw Stephanie twice and then asked her parents back to my office so that I could tell them what I had discovered about their daughter from her visits, and also so that I could ask them some questions that had arisen out of those visits. I knew that they, too, would have more questions for me. Finally, if they agreed to therapy, we needed to talk about plans for Stephanie's treatment.

The series of visits that led up to Stephanie beginning treatment was fairly typical of what's known as a consultation—four visits, two with the parents and two with the child. Some therapists see the child first, either alone or with his parents; as you read on, you'll see why I prefer to meet just the parents initially.

But first, let me tell you some more about the various phases of consultation, so that you can understand why they're necessary, how best to use the parent visits, and how to introduce your child to the fact that he is going to be visiting a "worry doctor," as child therapists sometimes call themselves.

I should point out here that a consultation with a therapist doesn't have to center around the question "Does my child need treatment?" Sometimes parents need professional advice because they feel that something momentous has happened or is going to happen in a child's life and they want guidance on how to handle it. It could be that you are about to be divorced; it could be the recent death of someone close to the child; it could even be that a new baby is soon to be born. These kinds of events, as parents know, can have a powerful impact on the way a child feels and functions emotionally, depending on how they're handled. Later in this chapter I'll tell you about the one-shot, preventative consultation that allows parents to come in without their child, simply to ask for advice and get suggestions from someone who understands how children respond to these kinds of crises.

THE FIRST PARENT VISIT

As Stephanie's story suggests, the purpose of the first visit is for parents and therapist to get to know one another, and for the therapist to get to know something about the child and his parents' concerns about him. I believe that it's best if a child is not a part of this first meeting. It's up to the parents to decide, "This person's okay to treat my child," before the child is ever subjected to a first interview. Otherwise you are asking a young and upset person to meet someone with whom he might be expecting to form a relationship, only to then be taken to someone else because you didn't like this therapist.

For both therapist and parent, then, the first visit is for the purpose of evaluation. The therapist will begin to evaluate your child's need for treatment, and you will begin to evaluate the therapist. But how can a parent begin to evaluate a professional in the specialized field of child therapy? Basically, it's a matter of knowing what to ask yourself about the therapist, and what to ask the therapist about herself.

What to Ask Yourself

The first thing to consider in evaluating a therapist is, "How do I feel in the room with this person?" I can't stress enough how important this is, because it strongly affects the success of parent-work—the collaborative working relationship of parent and child therapist—and in my opinion, parent-work is one of the most important elements in a child's treatment.

You are going to be working very closely with the therapist. Does she respect your values? Is she willing to try to work around important family traditions or customs, and to consider your personal priorities? Or does she rigidly impose her view on you? Is she considerate of your limitations—emotional or practical—in the recommendations she makes, or does it seem to you that she's asking you to do things that are impossible? You should have a sense that the therapist is respectful of who you are, as a person—otherwise you'll probably always be working along different and irreconcilable tracks.

There could be just one little thing in this person's manner that troubles or irritates you. Before you decide to ignore that nagging detail, you might want to reflect on it briefly and make sure it's not the kind of thing that over a period of time could get in the way of a good working relationship. You don't have to have an immediate intimacy with the therapist, but you should have a sense that this is someone you can comfortably confide in, and whose judgment you respect.

On the other hand, in thinking about how comfortable you feel with the therapist, you should also examine how much your evaluation is affected by the feelings that you have about seeking treatment for your child. Some parents are very anxious about what they're going to hear from the therapist; there's a tendency to try to shield oneself from hearing the worst, by telling oneself in advance that this person has no understanding. This can be especially true if therapy was not your idea. If you were referred by your child's school, for instance, you might easily come to your meeting convinced that both the school and the therapist are wrong about your child, and that you as his parent understand him better than anyone outside the family.

Many parents begin to feel very ashamed when they're faced with a sense of exposure at their first consultation with a child therapist. Perhaps you've been playing down your child's problems to friends and relatives, but now you have to describe to the therapist all of the behavior problems and how you've been dealing with them, and an authoritative evaluation is about to be handed back to you. For some parents this can seem like a very supportive experience—finally, here's someone who can help. But there are many others who find this aspect of consultation very uncomfortable.

Don't go home thinking that these should remain your private feelings; any feelings you have about your child or your child's treatment need to be shared with the therapist so that something constructive can be done with them. Use the opportunity of the consultation to discuss, clarify, and hopefully begin to resolve your initial doubts and fears if you feel that this is somebody you want to work with.

Child-Therapist Match

Is my child going to like this person? Obviously, this is the other very important thing to consider in evaluating a therapist.

Again, it's largely a question of match. And again, you have to examine your own feelings and see how they're influencing your ideas. It's a matter of differentiating your own feelings and preferences from those of your child. You yourself may like a person with the kind of upbeat personality that comes across very strong, and yet your child might prefer someone who has a very gentle manner and gives him a lot of space.

As a parent, you know your child and the kind of person he relates to most easily. One mother who came to see me, for instance, told me about a therapist she had consulted previously, and against whom she had decided to send her child. "You know, she was a nice lady," she said. "But she was very low-key, and there was nothing in her manner that would have reached out and brought my child in." This was a child who was very reserved and a little frightened, and probably needed a more lively and playful person. But another child who was more outgoing might have been fine with this therapist. The other thing to remember is that some therapists are able to vary their way of relating to children, depending on what they see as the child's personality.

Your child will also have something to say about the therapist if he meets her. Stephanie, for example, didn't like people who "made her do things." She had been for a previous consultation with a therapist who asked her to draw pictures and play with certain toys, and had decided that she didn't want to be in treatment with this person. Mrs. Baker felt that her very rigid daughter needed someone more flexible if she was to settle in comfortably, and so she kept looking.

In my experience many children—and especially girls—are influenced in how they feel about a therapist by the way the person looks. They'll tell their parents, "I like her because she's pretty," "I don't like him—he's fat." It's important for a parent to remember that once a child begins to get to know a therapist, the chances are that the therapist's appearance will not be central to the relationship.

Parents often ask me whether a male or female therapist would be preferable for their child. In general, before adolescence, I would say that it makes no difference. But there are instances in which I would recommend one or the other. A child growing up with a single parent—a mother, for instance—might benefit from a close, substitute relationship with a male therapist. This is true whether the child is a boy or a girl. A boy with no father might need a male person to identify with; a girl can learn to grow close to a man, to like a man—someone around whom she can have the early romantic feelings that little girls usually focus on their fathers.

The other instance where a male or female therapist might be preferable is when powerful conflicts need to be worked out between a child and a parent of a particular gender. One six-year-old boy whose parents consulted me was clearly very angry at females. At this point in his life, all his constructive energy was invested in what it means to grow up to be a man, and he wanted women out of his life. That's where he was; that was the flow of his development, and at the end of the consultation I told his parents, "Look, you'd be going against the current to give him a female therapist. Let him have a male." On the other hand, once in a while a therapist will say, "This child has so many difficulties with women, let him have a woman to work them out with." The judgment can be made by the consulting therapist.

Essential Qualities

Besides your own personal feelings and the match with your child, there are certain personal qualities that you should look for in a child therapist, and the main thing is a general sense of warmth and thoughtfulness. You will also want to get a sense that this person is experienced in dealing with children, and has a real understanding of what it is to be a child.

What to Ask the Therapist

Assuming that you like this therapist, it's a good idea to use the first session to ask the kind of questions whose responses would immediately eliminate the therapist from your list of potential professionals. After all, why bother to bring your child in if her fees are way beyond what your budget can allow? Some of the major issues you might be concerned about are: What are the therapist's credentials? (You can find out more about what these credentials mean in terms of training and approach in Appendix A.) What's her background in child treatment? How available is this person to parents, in terms of phone contact and parent meetings? What's her policy regarding confidentiality for children? Will she keep you informed as to how treatment is going?

Some parents ask me what my theoretical approach is. In answering this question, I always wonder what's really on the parent's mind. Very often, for example, people feel that if a therapist has a Freudian approach, it means that she'll shut the parent out and scarcely talk to the child. These are misconceptions that can trouble a parent. It's important to make clear to a therapist what your real worry is; if you frame your anxieties in a theoretical question, you might receive a highly theoretical answer that's meaningless to a layman when, for example, all you really want to know is, "Can I call you when I'm worried between sessions?"

If your child has a specific disorder or handicap—for instance, if he has been categorized as having Attention Deficit Disorder, or if he's mentally retarded—then you should find out if the therapist has any special expertise in this area (this is a question you might like to ask on the phone when you make your first contact). You're also very free to ask the therapist what her experience is with your child's particular problem—what has been her experience treating children with school phobia, for instance, or with encopresis, if these things are plaguing your child.

What the Therapist Will Ask You

When I see parents for an initial consultation meeting, I hope to be "introduced" to their son or daughter in a way that will frame my first meeting with the child. I always start by asking, "What brings you here today?" Through the parents' answer I hope to get a picture of the current problem, some background on the problem, how they've been dealing with it, and how the child is functioning in all the important areas of his life. Who is this person? What's he like to live with? How does he make friends? I sometimes ask a little about birth history and infancy, particularly if I feel it's relevant, but I'm much more interested initially in getting the current picture and the current problem, and hearing about where it all started.

Sometimes parents minimize problems in their own minds. One set of parents never mentioned to me that for two years their small boy had been refusing to cooperate in the classroom. His parents thought that this was just who he was and at times they were proud of his spirit; but in fact the child was having a horrible time in school. Try to think about and describe your child not only as you see her, but as others see her, too. If the school says she's impossible to deal with but you find her perfectly charming at home, tell the therapist this; if other children don't want to play with her because in their opinion she's mean or aggressive, yet you've never seen her as such and you believe her friends are just ganging up on her, this is also something the therapist needs to know.

By the end of your first visit, you'll probably know whether or not you want to work with this person, and the therapist will know whether or not she needs to see your child. As I've said, with problems that seem practical or circumscribed—like how to prepare a child for divorce, or how to get your child to stay in bed at night—I can usually give advice without having to see children. In situations when a child visit is called for, I'll give the parents some idea of why I think this is necessary. This doesn't mean that I can tell parents all sorts of things they didn't already know about their son or daughter. Sometimes I get a very clear picture from what a parent tells me about a child in the first visit, but other children are more of a puzzle to me, and I need the insight I can get through playing with the child or talking to him.

THE CHILD VISITS

Who is she? What's she going to do? What am I going to have to do? What should I tell her? These are the kinds of questions your child might ask you when you tell him that he's going to be visiting a therapist.

When I set up consultation appointments for children, the parents always ask me, "How shall I tell him?" A therapist will probably want to advise you on how to answer your child's questions, because the way in which the child is introduced to her before they even meet will color the all-important therapist-child relationship.

How to Introduce Your Child to the Idea of Therapy

As I always tell parents, how you introduce your child to the idea of therapy really depends, first of all, on the age of the child and how much he can understand. Usually a very young child really needs some superficial answer so that he doesn't feel he's in a vacuum. In general, I ask parents to present me as a helping person, and I ask them to explain to the child the kinds of things with which I can help him. If your child has a specific problem, you can tell him that the therapist is there to help him deal with it, but only if the child himself sees it as a problem and wants to overcome it. No child, for instance, likes to be frightened by monsters in his bedroom, and many are eager to do something about bed-wetting so that they can feel free to sleep over at a friend's house. A child who can't make friends might respond well to the suggestion that here's someone who can help him understand something about friendship—if he's expressed an interest in making friends.

But a child who's just plain oppositional or aggressive isn't going to respond very positively to the suggestion that this person called a therapist is going to help him stop yelling at Mommy, or stop giving the teacher a hard time. On the other hand, the child who's always fighting at home might see some sense in talking to someone who can help things be better between himself and his parents. The more uncomfortable a child is about something, the more it makes sense for him to come.

What Happens During the Child Sessions

Stephanie walked into my office, followed by her mother with my permission. She looked around apprehensively and started to chat very anxiously and condescendingly about how weird and stupid the things in my office were. It's quite normal for a child to be anxious in this situation, but Stephanie's condescending attitude already told me something about her: When things made her anxious, she needed to protect and elevate herself by demeaning them in some way. She had been responding in the same way to her anxieties over weekend trips with her family; she would say that she hated this or that place or person.

Stephanie talked about some distant relatives, and then told me that a room in my dollhouse was sloppy while she, on the other hand, liked to keep things neat and make her bed and she was a good girl. She felt the need to aggrandize herself and put me down. Every time I told her something, she would say, "I know, I know." Many children say this in an attempt to appear intelligent, but the impatient tone of her voice, combined with the other signs she was giving me, suggested that Stephanie felt the need to maintain the upper hand at all costs, because she felt so badly about herself.

It's during my initial meetings with the children themselves that I really start to find out about them, although this is in no sense a structured interview. I know that many children aren't able to talk about things right away, so I assess the situation before bringing up any charged or uncomfortable issues. If I feel that this child is frightened about being in my room, my emphasis is on helping him to feel comfortable with me and learning what I can in the gentlest possible way. I knew from what Stephanie's parents had told me, for example, that this child would be much more forthcoming if I allowed her to offer information, rather than if I came at her with structured questions.

Some children love to talk, and tell me all their problems almost immediately. One little four-year-old came to see me, and after we'd been playing at the dollhouse for a while, she told me, "You know, I hate myself." At first she gave me a very evasive answer as to why, but as I saw her relax and warm up, I asked her again, and she said, "Because I'm so angry my mother went back to work, and because I'm so angry, it makes me feel like a bad person."

Once in a while it's very important for my recommendation that I do find something out, and then I might ask the child more questions, in a way that doesn't seem too threatening—parents know how resistant children are to talking about the thoughts and feelings that they've been trying to protect themselves against. I give the child a "TV remote-control" button (it's really just a piece of wood with two bumps on it) that I keep in my office. I tell the child that I'm going to ask some questions, and that if any of the questions make him uncomfortable enough that he doesn't want to answer, he need only point the remote at me and switch me off. It works beautifully, because it provides a safety valve for children. It helps them to tolerate the discomfort of being questioned, because they know they can stop it at any time; they're in control. Children usually find this "power" great fun.

Why Two Visits?

Children respond in different ways to their first and second visits, and these differences can tell me quite a lot. The first time I see a child, he's under stress, so I get a sense of how he responds to a less familiar situation. The second time I see the child, I get a better sense of his coping skills and how effectively he'll be able to use the process of therapy. Does he remember things from the last time? Is he still anxious, or has he mastered his anxiety in some way and adapted to the situation? Can he make himself comfortable when something is more familiar, or am I still a stranger to him? These things are just as important to me as the things a child tells me as we talk.

I was consulted once about a ten-year-old girl who was in a state of fright after her house had been broken into and burglarized. On the basis of her parents' descriptions during their first visit with me, I felt that their daughter would probably be fine with some short-term therapy. I asked to see her, and when I saw how very tense and compliant this girl was, I started to doubt my original assessment. But the second time this child came in to see me, she responded quite differently. She asked if she could sit in a different place that felt better to her; she had questions to ask about me, my office, and about herself. In the second visit I saw strengths in her that would allow me to recommend short-term work after all.

Judging from two visits and parent information, I can generally formulate a recommendation as to whether or not treatment would be advisable, and also how well treatment might work for the child. If the child manages to connect with me, to open up and tell me things or to play out his anxieties in some way, then I can hazard a guess that therapy will work faster here than for the child who remains completely closed and distant. If both visits are extremely painful, I might decide that the child would benefit more from another form of treatment, for instance with parents and child in the room together.

THE SECOND PARENT VISIT

By the second visit of the consultation, I was able to give Stephanie's parents some feedback on how I saw her in consultation, what I thought the problem was in a general sense, and what I recommended. I explained why Stephanie needed more consistent limits, and how Stephanie was being given too much authority in her life and too much freedom to play out her anxieties instead of being encouraged to get past them. I recommended treatment, with two weekly sessions and regular parent contact.

Listening to the Evaluation—Painful Feelings

If faced with the therapist's diagnosis and recommendations at the second meeting you begin to feel that the therapist is being judgmental or rigid, you should try to sort out for yourself whether you're feeling this way because of who she is, or because of your own anxieties and shame at what she's telling you.

You have to expect this to be a difficult visit. All sorts of painful feelings can arise, like shame, guilt, or even a denial that there's any problem at all. You might have been feeling these things for quite some time as you watched your child getting into trouble, or put up with his embarrassing public tantrums, and yet now all the pain and guilt comes rushing to the surface as your worst fears are confirmed. As you work with the therapist, however, you'll begin to form a clearer picture of your child's problems, and they might start to seem much less serious than you had secretly imagined.

Quite often one parent wants to go ahead with therapy, while the other thinks it's a waste of time, or that an outsider can't help with the problem. The father of one four-year-old, who had been referred to me by the child's school, was obviously very disappointed and angry when I recommended treatment for his child. He had clearly been hoping that I would simply be able to give him some basic advice and send him away, without his very troubled son ever having to enter treatment. In his eyes, this was something that ought to be taken care of in the family. I believe that when a parent feels strongly that the solution to a child's problem can only be found within the family, that parent is in fact trying to normalize the problem: "If we handle it, then it means that our child is normal. But if she enters therapy, then we have to officially acknowledge a problem, one that we might have created."

This kind of feeling, which combines guilt and the fear of having a disturbed child, is something to discuss in consultation. The therapist might tell you that what's needed is a collaborative effort; few children can be helped by a therapist alone, without the parents' active participation. In the chapter on Parent-Work, I'll talk more about how a therapist can, during the course of your child's treatment, help you deal with these kinds of painful feelings.

Mapping Out the Course of Action

When I recommend treatment, I usually tell parents why I'm recommending it, which areas I feel need working on, and where I think treatment can be of most help (therapy works better in some areas than in others). I told Stephanie's parents, for instance, that I thought we needed to work on her overdependency on her mother. I explained that in many cases I deal with this kind of attachment by helping the child to move out of that relationship toward the next closest place—the relationship with the father—and by helping to make that place feel safe. I suggested to Stephanie's father how he could help in this by making an effort to develop his relationship with her at home.

On the other hand, when I consulted with four-year-old Betty's mother, I explained to her that therapy cannot make the outbursts of her temperamentally impulsive child go away. What I could do to help her daughter was work with her on preventing some of the outbursts by understanding the triggers, and I could help her find ways of calming down more quickly. The same is true of the outbursts that are so typical of children with Attention Deficit Disorder.

It sometimes happens that the problem I see is different from the problem the parents initially came to see me about. Mark's parents, for instance, felt that his problem centered around aggression and anger, because he was going around bullying everyone. But I saw the aggression as this boy's way of handling a fragile sense of self. At the age of three and a half, he was waking up every night crying, "I'm nobody"; he refused all offers of consolation or help (he couldn't stand to be helped because it made him feel weak); he laid down the law at home in the most rigid, arbitrary way, and had tantrums if he wasn't obeyed. His parents were surprised by my evaluation, but it gave them a better understanding of their son and how they could help him.

I'm sometimes able to learn something new about a child during consultation, something that the parents never noticed or ceased paying attention to long ago. After all, parents are with their children every day and get so used to certain behaviors that they just don't think about them anymore. One boy's parents, for instance, who had been referred to me by a psychological tester looking at the possibility of learning disabilities, had described him during our first meeting as being very friendly and outgoing. And yet when I saw the boy, I noticed that although there was a surface friendliness if I didn't get too close, he had a great deal of anxiety about being alone in the room with me. He wouldn't tell me his mother's name, and got silly and anxious when I asked him his stepfather's name.

This gave me several questions to ask the boy's parents at our next meeting. I had to find out about the quality of his relating. Who was he really close to besides his parents? Who could he be left alone with? Was he able to ask for help? I found out that, in fact, there were real problems when it came to this boy's relationships with anyone besides his parents. This was definitely something that we needed to work on.

Of course, the goals of treatment have to be decided between the therapist and the parents; there's no use in my trying to encourage a child to be more aggressive so that he'll stand up for himself if the parents really like him to be sensitive and yielding. I have to try to find some common ground that's in the interests of the child and that the parents can agree to. Also, at this point parents can discuss with the therapist any requests they might have about how therapy is framed for their child. Paul's mother, for instance, told me that she would like her son to have a sense that he was entering therapy regarding a problem that was the family's and not his alone. I felt that she was absolutely right in feeling that this sensitive boy should not have to bear the burden of feeling that he was the problem in the relationship between himself and his mother. Treatment was explained to Paul as a cooperative effort to deal with problems in the family. I worked on it with him during his visits, and I would work with his parents on it, too.

Predicting the Length of Treatment

Parents often ask me how long treatment is likely to take. Unfortunately, it's really impossible during the consultation stage to predict how many sessions a child will need, but I can usually give parents some basic guidelines. For instance, I've found that circumscribed problems around a specific issue, such as divorce, tend to need relatively short-term treatment, as does a problem that's fairly recent in its origin. On the other hand, when parents tell me, "Oh, she's always been like this," I generally foresee a longer course of treatment.

Another way I have of getting some general sense of how long treatment could last is by looking at the goals. If the child needs my help in overcoming some kind of conflict or upset in his life, or in his way of seeing these issues, then treatment is likely to be short. But when some area of that child's personality has never developed, then it may well take longer. Stephanie is a good example. There were certain areas of her personality that had never developed: her sense of autonomy, as well as her ability to regulate her self-esteem and to tolerate separations so that life outside her house could be fulfilling. Some children, like Betty, have to develop their power to regulate their own impulses. As I work with a child and get to know him, I develop a better sense of how he'll respond to treatment, and how long it will take before he's grown enough to function in the world without my help.

Practical Matters

If treatment is recommended, now's the time to ask some of the questions that concern the format of your child's course of therapy: How many times per week will he be seeing the therapist? When should the child begin treatment, especially if there are vacations coming up? What's the billing system? What is the therapist's policy on canceled appointments—in other words, will you have to pay even though your child is sick and can't make it to his session? How often will she want to see you, the parents, separately or together? All these questions should be clarified by the end of the consultation, before your child enters treatment.

A Note on Consultation and Divorced Parents

Mrs. Foster called me one day to set up an appointment for a consultation about her daughter. She told me that her ex-husband was away on a business trip and that she didn't want to wait for his return before coming to see me. Instead, she wanted to come with the child's stepparent, who, she said, was more like a real father to her by this point anyway.

I had already experienced several instances in which a divorced parent—especially a parent who felt shut out of his child's life when an ex-spouse sidestepped him in the consultation process—decided to refuse permission for the child's treatment, and so I told Mrs. Foster that I preferred to wait for her ex-husband to return before setting up an appointment. Sure enough, a couple of weeks later I had a call from her to say that her ex-husband had returned and was opposed to the idea of therapy for their daughter. Had we already entered the consultation process, this little girl's therapy would have become an issue between her divorced parents, only adding to her pain.

I always tell parents who are divorced that I prefer to see them for consultation together with their ex-spouses if it's at all possible for them, so that the child can see therapy as something that both parents agree on, however much animosity exists between them. If a joint appointment isn't feasible, then I try to see them both within the same week. Even if a parent is remarried, I prefer to see the biological, rather than the stepparent first in the interests of establishing the fact that the child's therapy is supported by both parents. As it is, the noncustodial parent often feels left out, and no therapist wants to perpetuate that feeling through the child's treatment.

THE ONE-TIME PREVENTATIVE CONSULTATION

Parents are quite free to consult therapists in a preventative context—in other words, to seek advice on how to deal with something that is about to happen, or has just happened in the child's life, so that difficult responses can be minimized. I'm often consulted by parents who are on the brink of divorce, for instance, and who are worried about how the children will respond. This kind of consultation often consists of a single meeting, with the opportunity to follow up by phone or in person should the need arise. Because the contact with the therapist will not be weekly or sustained, and because there's no long-term financial commitment, you'll probably be less concerned with how comfortable you feel with this person, and with practical issues such as fees or proximity.

I should make the point here that when you go for a one-shot consultation with a therapist, you're likely to feel inundated with advice, and may even be presented with a step-by-step plan of action to be followed at home. In my experience, parents find it much easier to absorb and retain all this information if they come prepared to take notes.

What Kinds of Problems Can Be Dealt With in a One-Time Consultation?

Although the most common issues around which I'm consulted on a one-time basis are divorce and the arrival of a new baby in the family, I have also seen parents who needed to know how to deal with a variety of specific, troubling incidents. Some parents, for instance, wanted to know if there was anything more they could do to help their child deal with an incident of sexual abuse. Another set of parents came to see me for advice on how to prepare their child, who had some separation problems, for the death of a very ill grandparent; even if a child isn't close to a relative, just the fact of death being brought home can set off the idea that he might suddenly lose people who are close to him. Parents know their children, and are able to foresee when a specific event is likely to cause them trouble.

Consulting About Babies and Toddlers

Another area in which a therapist can help through one-time consultation is by offering advice to parents of babies and young toddlers, who are generally seen as too young to need or respond to individual treatment. A child therapist can help with issues such as toilet training, how to parent a "difficult" baby so that problems will be less likely to emerge later, and what form of caretaking is appropriate.

The mother of an eighteen-month-old boy wanted some help in making a difficult caretaking decision. The baby had had so many different baby-sitters ever since he was born that she didn't really want to change again, yet she was very unhappy with the woman who was looking after him at this point. Although I usually feel that consistency in caretaking is more important than finding the ideal caretaker, this particular sitter was so far from ideal that I recommended a change. Although the baby wasn't acting unusually clingy, or crying when he was left with the sitter—sure signs that something is wrong—he was reportedly very quiet with her. In fact, it turned out that in advising a caretaking change I was supporting the intuition of the baby's mother; she simply needed a professional to confirm what she felt was right, and she needed advice on how to introduce the new sitter in such a way that the baby would not feel too much at sea. "Let's do it in the best way possible," I said. "Can you find a time when you can take a week off work so that you're there with the new caretaker while your baby grows familiar with her?" This was the basis of the plan, and all went well, although as you'll see, the parents had further questions for me around this issue.

Consulting About Divorce

When parents come to see me about an impending divorce, they usually want to know how to announce it to their child: Under what circumstances should they tell him? What would be the best day? What should they say or not say? My job is to help them understand how best to prepare their child for an event that is bound to have a powerful impact on his life. Since no two children are the same, I rely on the parents to tell me something about the youngster; a therapist's advice should be tailor-made.

When do you break the news to children? Is it best to tell them when they'll be going to school, so they have something to take their mind off it, or on a weekend, so they can be home where they can show their feelings and be reassured by the family? I usually feel that it's better for a child to be home, although after a day or two it can be a good idea for him to go on with his normal life—returning to school on Monday, for instance, is fine for most kids.

Besides giving advice on the announcement itself, I try to offer suggestions on how to prepare children for the physical moving out of a parent. I believe that, if possible, the parent who is moving out should have at least a temporary new home so that the child can see where this parent is going to be living, and have some kind of mental picture in his head of where the absent parent is. Without this, it's easy for children to feel as if a father, or mother, has suddenly fallen off the face of the earth. It's an even greater help to a child if he can see the room where he's going to sleep when he visits the parent, and maybe even leave something there, like a toy or a favorite doll.

For the sake of the children involved in a divorce, I always advise parents to try and maintain some kind of control over themselves during these times of stress, however difficult it may be to do so. It's fine to let a child see that you're sad and upset, but if you let yourself fall apart, your child can become frightened, especially at a time when he's suffering an emotional blow and needs your support.

In my opinion, the most important thing you can do to help a child through a divorce is to understand his reactions, and not to be scared by them, or to be so overwhelmed with guilt that you're unable to act in the best interests of your child. You have to allow a child the freedom to express his upset by what is, indeed, a tumultuous event in his life—and yet at the same time you have to try not to overcompensate.

How can a parent tell what is reasonable behavior in a child going through a divorce? I always tell parents, "You can let him cry, mope, tell off a particular parent, or ask important but sensitive questions, but you shouldn't permit him to act in ways that are destructive to himself or to others, or for which he'll have to pay a price later." In other words, although you should let your child know that you understand that when he's sad it's hard for him to pay attention in school, you shouldn't let him neglect homework that you know he's really not too upset to do.

Consulting About the Birth of a Sibling

"I'm pregnant and my little girl can't get enough attention as it is—how can I prevent problems arising after the baby's born?" "When my child needs me and I'm busy with the baby, how do I tell him that I can't deal with him right now?" These are the kinds of issues that a therapist can help you with in consultation. In my experience, it's really a matter of preparing a situation in which the child feels perfectly free to express his feelings about the baby's arrival. Parents sometimes expect their children to act especially grown up as new big brothers or sisters. In fact, many small children in particular feel quite the opposite during this life crisis. It's up to a parent to give a child some kind of reassurance, both spoken and unspoken, that he is free to regress, to need you more, once the baby comes. Even children who never forgive a new sibling for its arrival can usually get to the point where they don't allow these negative feelings to interfere with other parts of their lives.

Follow-Up

You needn't feel as if you've been thrown into the deep end after a one-shot consultation with a child therapist. When parents consult me about a specific issue, I always tell them, "Why don't you go home and try these things for a while, and then call and let me know how things are going. Or call sooner if you have questions." Therapists generally welcome this kind of feedback.

3

꙰

A LOOK THROUGH
THE WINDOW:
PLAY THERAPY

When someone asked a five-year-old patient of mine, David, what he was doing after school, he replied, "I'm going on a play date with a grown-up."

Our play date, one of two regular weekly visits, consisted of about forty-five minutes of play and talk. While we played, David's mother waited outside my office, no doubt wondering what was going on inside and hoping that it would work. David's rages, at home and at school, were making life a nightmare for everyone. She had started David in treatment in September, as he entered kindergarten, because the boy was clearly out of control and neither she nor her husband had been able to put things right.

One of the first things I tell parents about play therapy is that I need their active collaboration in their child's treatment, because the time that children spend with me each week is insignificant in comparison with the time spent at home and at school. In my experience, the involvement of parents—what I call parent-work—is central to the success of a child's treatment in play therapy, and yet as a parent it can be hard to reconcile the need to be involved with the fact that you have very little idea of what's going on during your child's session. Without watching the process, it's also very difficult to understand how play can help your child. I hope this chapter will open a window into the play-therapy room, so that you can get a sense of the kinds of things that happen during child treatment, and of how play acts as a vehicle through which children express their hurts and confusions.

Apart from the confidential nature of my play date with David, playing in the therapy office was not so different, on the surface, from playing at a friend's house. In some ways it was probably easier for him. When he had play dates with friends, he tended to get into trouble for flying into a rage or lashing out; this child's self-esteem was so fragile that he would fall apart at the slightest insult. His only way of feeling strong, in his childlike way, was to scream and bully. But getting into trouble over his tantrums only made him feel worse about himself.

In the therapy room, on the other hand, there were no parents to get upset or mad at David's behavior, and there were no fights over who wanted to play what. David was free to choose what he wanted to play with; the toys in my office are all within easy reach of children so that they can walk in, decide what they want to play, and take if off the shelf.

Quite often David chose action figures. In the beginning of treatment, he had the bad guys, I had the good guys, and the bad guys always won because David made up the rules. Occasionally he wanted to play with dolls, pretending to be interested in the mechanical aspects as he carefully examined Barbie. One of his favorite games was Connect Four, but he usually cheated because he couldn't stand to lose. Because I was still trying to help

David get comfortable in treatment, I simply observed his cheating as a measure of how desparately he needed to win. But, as I tell parents, my role is very different from the parental role. A parent needs to be firm with a child who cheats (unless, of course, she's very young, in which case all it takes is a reminder). A child of school age has to be told, "I'm not going to play with you unless you play by the rules."

Sometimes David decided to play alone; when that happened, I became, instead of a playmate, an interested but unobtrusive observer. Of course, play dates are seldom all play, and nor were ours. David had been coming to my office regularly for a few months, and while play tended to be the core of our forty-five-minute sessions, there was a lot more besides. Occasionally David drew, or sometimes we just sat and chatted, although David had evidently made a deliberate decision never to engage in or permit any talk about himself or his life. I understood this to be his way of controlling the situation, by not giving me what he felt I wanted, so that he could feel strong and good about himself in one of the few ways available to him. Although for a long time our relationship was soothing and supportive, it never touched on deeper issues.

One of the things I wanted was for David to bring his rages to me. I wanted him to be able to have a tantrum in my office, to show me how upset he was, so that I could better understand the triggers to his tantrums, help him find better ways of dealing with his uncomfortable feelings, and show him that I accepted those aspects of his personality about which he felt so ashamed.

But he was too afraid to let me see that side of him; he felt that nobody could love the obnoxious child he felt himself to be. I knew that David's mother had jokingly called him Oscar the Grouch, so I went and bought a Grouch doll and had it in my office the next time David came to play. Then, for many sessions, we argued playfully about whether or not anybody could possibly love such a miserable character as Oscar, and whether

angry Oscar could ever love someone else. David's v{
bled with powerful feelings of despair as he told me, "'
love Oscar! Get him out of here!"

WHAT IS PLAY THERAPY?

Play is only one aspect of what is broadly known as play therapy, a form of child treatment based on using play as the child's
means of expressing and sometimes working through conflicts.
In fact, many kinds of things can go on in the therapy room, and
all of them are useful because whatever a child chooses to do
during sessions helps me to come to an understanding of her
world. Only with this understanding can I go on to offer her a
way out of her difficulties, and can I share my insights with her
parents, so that they can play their part in putting things right.

Learning Through the Relationship

I often learn most about a child through the relationship she
builds with me, and the real-life experiences that happen while
we're together in the room. Generally these experiences occur
naturally through the relationship we develop around play,
allowing the child to work through problems of relating, and
giving me the opportunity of answering some essential questions:
How easily can she trust me? Is she afraid to like me? How can
she be comforted when she has a tantrum? Sometimes revealing
things happen in the relationship around play. David, for instance, would fly into a rage whenever I beat him in a board
game; he was incapable of sustaining a loss. Sometimes just a
small incident will tell me as much. If Susie asks to keep a toy
and, while trying to understand her wish I have to disappoint
her by saying that the toys can't be taken home, how does she
react?

I look at how a child copes. As events occur naturally while
we're in the room together, I get a sense of the mechanisms he

has developed for dealing with day-to-day difficulties. Is he coping with his fears by trying to keep everything and everyone tightly within his control, as Stephanie did with her family when she refused to leave the house on family trips? I try to help children find new ways of coping. Knowing that taking toys can be a child's way of easing the separation by bringing a piece of the office home with her, I might ask her, "Is there some other way you might feel better about saying good-bye?"

These are just some of the things I look for in the relationship a child develops with me in the course of treatment. Perhaps most important, I try to find out how he perceives himself and his limited world of family and friends. Whether he is playing alone or with me, or we're talking, or he's having a tantrum, or he's resisting any kind of contact, for a couple of hours each week I live out his life with him.

The Language of Play

Why, then, do we call this play therapy? First of all, as every adult knows, play is the most effective way of building trusting relationships with most children. From birth, children relate to others through play. You might jingle a bunch of keys to elicit a smile from an infant, or watch as your five-year-old quickly becomes friends with another child he just met over a game of tag. Even the relationship between child and parent, founded first of all on nurturing, is enriched by play. In therapy as in daily life, play serves initially as as a vehicle through which therapist and child can get to know each other, and as a way of putting children at ease, so that they can relax and open up.

Most important of all, play is a major form of expression for children. Pioneers of therapy for children based their work on the idea that children with emotional troubles are struggling with buried, unconscious conflicts resulting from powerful but unacceptable impulses, and that these conflicts must be revealed if the children are to be helped. This was the beginning of child analysis.

Instead of asking children to lie on the couch and talk about their feelings, as in adult analysis, many pioneers of child treatment developed techniques, based primarily on play, for helping children to reveal their conflicts, recognizing that children are too young to understand, or to describe in words, their troubled emotions.

Today, child analysis is a very specialized and intensive branch of child therapy. The child undergoing analysis sees a specially trained clinician four or five times a week, and treatment tends to last over a long period of time.

These days, play therapy has become a very broad term, and several models have been developed that, although they use some of the play techniques developed by child analysts, are quite different from analysis. Although many play therapists view themselves as working within the psychoanalytic model, in most instances play therapy today tries to help children with levels of feeling that are more easily brought into their awareness, and that affect them in their daily lives, rather than those that are deeply buried or more symbolic.

My own feeling is that while all troubled children do have conflicts underlying their difficulties, and some are best helped by focusing on the conflicts, many other children may need different kinds of help. When I work with a child, I'm interested in finding out what's on her mind; that is, not only if there are conflicts, but what her sense of self is, how she experiences and internalizes relationships, and also what kinds of real-life issues are making it hard for her to function or develop in her world. How can she be helped to function, to develop, to have friends, to learn, without neccessarily smoothing out every kink in her personality? Sometimes very practical work is needed to get a child, especially a phobic one, unstuck.

You may remember Jack, the "difficult child" from chapter

1. This boy came to me with many phobias and fears. But those fears were not symbolic; they were real. They stemmed from Jack's tendency to avoid rather than tolerate his anxiety while meeting the challenge of frightening situations, and from his habit of fastening onto negative things—he never forgot a worrisome experience, and would link his fears to other, related experiences.

Initially, instead of looking for unconscious material in Jack's play, I helped him to master his most interfering fears. At the age of eight, he had to learn that he really could go upstairs to his room on his own; that he could flush the toilet without being in danger from the loud noise; that he could do all those things that had been impossible for him; and that in doing them, he would feel more in control of his life. In three months he made dramatic progress in this area through my gradually helping him build up tolerance of his anxieties. In the process he also built his trust in me, enabling him to honestly explore his emotions with me later, when he was ready for a different kind of work.

Play Therapy and the Whole Child

This was only the first phase of treatment, because Jack had other problems that had been indirectly caused by, or in some cases had encouraged, his development of phobias. Jack's view of himself as a weak child, his wish to remain a baby cared for by others, had to be understood and dealt with.

I often understand symptoms, such as Jack's phobias, or another child's toilet-training problems, in relation to the child's view of herself and her world. If a child has difficulties controlling herself, or giving up a bottle, or relating to other children, I ask myself why. What is the root of this child's problem? Jack obviously saw himself as someone who could not master situations; this couldn't be separated from his wish to remain a helpless young child, as he felt too weak to be any other way. He was paying a huge price in self-esteem. I had to help him feel better and stronger about himself, primarily through helping him to understand his feelings and to find ways of coping with situations that made him anxious, rather than by avoiding them.

WHY PLAY?

Even though I'm dealing with feelings that are closer to a child's daily awareness, that doesn't mean that those feelings are understood by the child, or that she accepts them as her own. Perhaps her emotions are too painful for her to own up to, as in David's case. Other children may be caught up in feelings that stem from misconceptions about why certain things might have happened, or what might be about to happen; the child who thinks he's the cause of his parents' divorce is an obvious example.

Some children are confused or conflicted in ways that they can't even begin to understand in words, let alone express. There are things that children can't really tell me are bothering them—not because the feelings are too buried, but because they just don't have the capacity to understand it themselves.

Expressing Through Play

There is a wonderful example of the kinds of things children can express through play in the story of Mary, the very angry little girl from a high-pressured, professional family with tight schedules that didn't leave much room for children to be upset, or demanding, or messy, or preoccupied. Mary would come to my office, week after week, and create doll families. There were mothers, fathers, aunts, and uncles, but there were no children in her families. She could never have told me in words that she felt as if she and her little brother were intruders in their own home, but her play reflected it.

Children, and especially young children, are limited in their ability to verbalize their complex feelings, and they are also limited in their ability to make logical connections. Mary, for instance, knew in some sense that she was angry, and she had some notion that her parents were not prepared to adjust their life-style to make room for her, the child. But she couldn't put the two things together, because at her age a child's ability to reason is relatively immature.

Even as children reach the age when language is no longer such a struggle, and they are more able to express nuances of feeling verbally, play remains their least deliberate and self-conscious form of expression.

HOW CHILDREN USE PLAY FOR EMOTIONAL HEALTH

Play is the natural language of childhood. It's every child's way of working things out for himself, and of resolving problems about himself or his world—not only in therapy, but throughout childhood.

Most parents are well aware of the educational value of certain kinds of play—for instance, that building blocks help children to develop their sense of balance and introduce them to spatial concepts; or that when your toddler presses you into repeated games of peek-a-boo, he's not trying to test your patience, he's just learning that things continue to exist when they're out of his sight.

Parents generally encourage children to play with learning toys and often play along or watch, ready to help the toddler fit a triangle into a triangular hole instead of a square one, or to admire a youngster's Lego castle. But in today's rush to educate children, the role of play in their emotional development may have been undervalued.

When your child gets involved in fantasy play, you might think he's "just playing," and pay no attention. Yet it is through fantasy play that your child makes sense of his world, compensates for his wants, and expresses his anxieties. A child's fantasy life has unlimited scope; with few or no props, it allows him to be anyone, do anything, go anywhere, to reorganize objective reality according to his needs. He uses his imagination to help him cope with many of the challenges—social, intellectual, and emotional—that he has to meet in the course of growing up.

Preparing for Events

Perhaps you've watched your young child earnestly examining her favorite bear, or her best friend, with a pretend stethoscope the day before she's due for her doctor's checkup; or you may have noticed the games of teacher becoming very frequent during the first, uneasy weeks of kindergarten.

Obviously, it's no coincidence. Children use fantasy play to rehearse roles or situations that they're apprehensive about, and sometimes even to prepare themselves for events that they're looking forward to (even positive events can be stressful). Children play mother and father games in preparation for grown-up life, give their dolls and stuffed animals countless birthday parties. Perhaps there has been talk of a trip; you might find your child sending his stuffed rabbit on a train ride. Given the time to prepare for events, children will help themselves through this kind of play, and adults, by watching, can keep in touch with what's occupying a child's mind. If he veers toward playing doctor, day after day for weeks, you can be sure there's a reason.

Trying Out Roles

Children also use fantasy play to try out different roles; to find out what it would feel like to be really wicked, to be a hero, to be in danger. When a child needs some relief from feeling like a helpless child with little control over events in his life, he can give himself instant power by becoming a parent, a cop, a teacher, or some other authority figure. When a child always insists on being the authority figure, I might take it as a possible signal that he may be feeling overly controlled in some way. Perhaps he needs the opportunity to make some nonparenting decisions of his own—the kind of decisions that a child can be allowed to make, such as which toys he can bring on a trip.

Compensating for Wants

This last example, about playing the authority figure, touches on another function of play in the child's emotional well-being. As children grow, they become increasingly aware of the things they lack. These might be personal qualities, such as strength or good looks, or they might be material things.

Through imaginative play, children can make up for their wants. A child who sees herself as less pretty than her friends can become, for a while, a beautiful princess; another child might always play the tough guy. I have watched children who, feeling deprived of a mother's affection, spend hours showering love upon a baby doll—the child in proxy.

Discharging Emotions

Most children eventually learn to regulate themselves in the face of those real and powerful angers, jealousies, and hates that they inevitably feel from time to time. Yet even the most self-controlled child, though he has learned not to give free rein to his unacceptable emotions, still feels the anger that makes him want to lash out.

Only in play can the child safely discharge some of her unacceptable emotions—and often it's in the kind of play that parents least favor. In games of fantasy, children get to be the revenger, the bad guy, they get to kill the enemy (parent), to torture the imposter (new baby), to wipe out every living inhabitant of the universe.

The beauty of fantasy play is that the basic tool—
imagination—is readily available to all children. Many of the
toys I have in my office—action figures; doll families and a
dollhouse, with play bottles and diapers; some props such as
policeman's hats and doctor's instruments, and domestic props
such as tiny pots and pans; a make-believe school—are intended
to encourage fantasy play. But they are not necessary. Children
naturally invent their own props, improvising with whatever
happens to be around. One of the favorite "toys" in my therapy
room happens to be my desk; children love to sit behind it and
feel big, pretending they're Daddy or Mommy at the office, or
they're the doctor and I'm the child patient.

A child's fantasy life has no need of grown-up help, and
there are no rules; in fact, the rules are invented and changed to
serve the child's emotional needs. In all my years of play therapy, I don't think I have once been allowed to win a game of good
guys versus bad guys. Every child I have played with has deftly
bent the rules as the game progressed, because the need to win
has been so strong. Children invent games to suit their need,
whether individually or among peers—when a group of kids
recently devised a new variation on tag called "kidnap," the
implications were clear. Built into this game, as in a fairy tale,
was the promise of escape from the captors.

Developing a Sense of Mastery

Not all of the toys in my office, however, are for fantasy play.
Board games, Legos, construction toys, and others that help
children to develop their skills can also have therapeutic value.

Activities that develop children's physical and cognitive
skills help them to achieve a sense of mastery. The greater their
sense of mastery, the firmer their self-esteem, and the more they
are able to feel that they have some control over their worlds. I
found that David, for example, could be calmed during a rage if,
while I stopped him from destroying anything, I taught him a

skill. The day I taught him how to use a telephone so that he could reach his father, I watched his confidence build as his sense of helplessness, and the tantrum, ebbed.

Activities designed for intellectual development can also be therapeutic in the sense that they help the child develop internal skills. Battling with Lego pieces can do a lot for frustration tolerance and perseverance; trying to shape a flower out of a piece of Play-doh that insists on looking like a modified lump can help a child to accept her own level of expertise in modeling, as long as the adults close to her accept the lump for what it is—a brave attempt and a beautiful flower.

Creating a Predictable World

From the youngest age, children use play as a way of solving problems and reassuring themselves about real, physical life. Many of the principles they discover in the process (often through trial and error), such as the fact that water always finds its own level, would be impossible to explain in words accessible to the child.

Three- or four-year-olds, for instance, who develop a passion for sorting objects into separate piles or boxes—all animals in one pile, all people in another, and so on—are giving order to the world around them. When children pour water into sand, or play in the mud, or wreck their paint sets by mixing all the colors together, they are finding out about the physical properties of materials. By gathering evidence to support or refute their budding theories, young children develop intellectually and at the same time make safer, more predictable worlds for themselves.

PLAY IN THERAPY

Given that children play at every available opportunity anyway—at home, in school, in the car, during dinner—you might

well ask, "Why should I send my child to go play with a therapist?" There are many answers. First, play—and especially
fantasy play—is on the whole a private language. But as a
therapist trained and experienced in the expressive language of
play as well as in the discipline of psychology, I am able to listen
to that language, and to speak to the child through it when I feel
he is ready to listen.

Also, children feel freer to express fantasy that relates to the
family when they're playing with a therapist, who is not associated with the child's ongoing struggles and conflicts in the way
parents are. Ironically, some of the most useful play moments
come at the point when the distinctions between home and
therapy blur, and the child starts transferring his more negative
feelings about the outside world onto his relationship with the
therapist.

Sometimes it's not enough to know how to read between the
lines of a child's play. Many children whom I see are so afraid to
let me see what they are really feeling that they guard themselves
from revealing anything about themselves. There's a special
kind of interaction that particularly lends itself to therapy, a
form through which children most readily reveal things that are
on their mind, but which for one reason or another they can't
directly communicate, as with David and Oscar the Grouch. I
call it "therapy in the third person."

The Third Person

Children often imbue stuffed animals, imaginary companions, or
other children with roles that really come from inside themselves. They put into something or someone else the feelings or
ideas that are troubling them, as a way of making themselves feel
safer, of taking the heat off themselves.

Children do it all the time: "She did it, not me." When a
small child brings me his bear to hug and admire, I know that
I'm really hugging and admiring the child himself; he's not ready

to ask me directly for my affection. When children start bringing their favorite toys to therapy, I take it as a sign that they're using this as a way of showing me something about themselves and their lives.

In therapy, children can talk about painful things, and I can respond, through their third-person proxies. Neither of us have to lay it on the table. A child might pull a baby doll off my shelf and talk about how scared it is, and we both know that the dependent baby is the child as she sees herself. Remember that when I bought the Oscar the Grouch doll for David, he identified with it immediately: "Get him out of the room!"

I told David that I liked Oscar, and he got very upset. "How can you like him? He's so grouchy, he doesn't like anything, he doesn't like anybody, he makes people mad!"

The doll had a secret heart hidden inside his mouth, and a shirt that said, LOVE A GROUCH. I suggested that maybe underneath some of the anger, Oscar really did have loving feelings, but he kept himself safe by trying to feel strong and angry and tough, so nobody could hurt him.

"Get him out of here! I can't stand him being here!" said David, and he hid the doll in the closet. But I said Oscar had to come out because I really liked him and understood him, and I knew he had all kinds of feelings.

"I can't stand to see you like him. He's so bad. We can't have him here!"

I told David I liked Oscar however he was, because I saw why he needed to be that way. Over the next few weeks we had many emotional conversations about this doll, and ultimately, after several sessions, David accepted Oscar's presence in the room. One day I even saw him pick up the doll and fondle it.

Through Oscar, David got a chance to express all his hurts, disappointments, and bitterness. He was able to tell me how unlovable he felt himself to be, and how he couldn't let himself hope that anybody could love him. And by talking about Oscar,

I managed to tell David all the things he hadn't before—that I understood, that I cared for him, *f* bring his rages to me and I would still care for him. later, David had his first tantrum in my office. He finally comfortable enough in his relationship with me to bring into my office the rages he had been having in the safety of his own home, enabling me to try and understand them.

The third person is a way of communicating something while protecting the self. When a child comes into my office and immediately tells me, "My friend was really, really bad in school today," I know that she is anxious to find out what I think of children who are naughty. When a little boy tells me, "This bear's mad because his mommy goes to work," he's clearly telling me why *he's* mad.

The boy has very creatively made his bear a proxy; my response has to be equally creative. Do I continue talking to him about his anger at his mother through the bear, or do I gently bring the feelings home to him? Knowing when, how, and whether to cross the barrier that a child has erected to protect herself from pain is one of the biggest decisions I have to deal with in treating children.

WHAT GOES ON IN THE THERAPY ROOM?

As I said in the beginning, play with toys and dolls is just one thing that happens during my play dates with children. Some children don't focus so readily on this kind of play (particularly older children who have begun to grow out of these activities). So I may employ a wide range of other activities in the therapy room.

Board Games. Playing board games with a child can offer me several insights. Are her strategies aggressive or cautious? How does he react to winning or losing? Is she confident about her skills, even when she does lose?

A lot of children I treat can't stand to lose a game. Every time they play, they're on the line. They become the outcome of the game; if they lose, they see themselves as hopeless losers. Some children get so anxious that they walk away from the game, or they start changing the rules or moving my pieces around.

Board games also offer children a way to keep busy while they chat to me about their lives. On the other hand, a child might try to use checkers or some other game to avoid revealing anything about herself during therapy. I always watch out for this, but if you find that your child has done nothing in therapy over a period of time but play checkers, for instance, you might want to ask the therapist whether anything useful is actually coming out of it.

Drawing. Like play, drawing is a wonderful form of self-expression for children of all ages, and child therapists are usually trained to understand something about the pictures children draw, besides their literal meaning.

I can often find out quite a bit about a child's perception of herself and her family through her drawings: Which member of the family is perceived as the tiniest, or the largest and most powerful looking? Who is the person with the prominent, predatorial teeth?

One boy who came to me for consultation was clearly angry with his mother, and interested in aligning himself with his father and the world of men. As I watched him draw his picture, starting with himself and his father, I could see that he was intending to draw his mother, too. But somehow he worked a door into the drawing next to the two men, and since the door was closed, there was no room to fit his mother in. "Gee," he said, "I guess there's nowhere to put my mother. But she's in there, she's behind the door."

If I think that the child can understand what she has re-vealed about herself through her drawing, I might comment on it by saying something like, "That child looks very tiny next to her friend. Does she think the friend is so much stronger?" Or "What little hands that girl has! I wonder if those little hands get to be a problem when she has to do something. Do you think they make her feel kind of helpless sometimes?" Sometimes, however, the drawing might be helpful only to me in my understanding of the child, and I keep the meaning to myself.

Dreams. I don't make a point of asking children about their dreams, although I might inquire during an initial consultation: "Are there any dreams that you especially remember and want to tell me about?" One seven-year-old girl I was seeing got a real kick out of interpreting her own dreams, and her father's, too. When a child is interested, dreams can be another way of learning about children.

Story Books. Story books are not traditional play-therapy fare, but I often find them quite useful in helping children to relax. Some books have themes that are very relevant to children's worries; there's nearly always something meaningful in a story around which I can get a child to chat about his feelings.

When I'm reading, I'll often stop mid-story and comment on some theme that I think is particularly meaningful to the child: "Oh! That daddy looks awfully angry! Why do you think he feels that way?" A quick remark like that can start a whole conversa-tion about daddies being angry. Essentially, this is a variation of therapy in the third person.

Expeditions. Sometimes, when children are having a particular-ly hard time coming to therapy, or something feels uncomfort-able about being alone with the therapist in a closed room for an entire session, I might suggest going out on an expedition. This doesn't happen often, and some therapists don't do it at all. But in my view (and many parents may share it) there are times when a walk, or a quick trip to get an ice-cream cone, can help enormously. Walking somehow fills the silence, and makes talking easier than when you're sitting across a table from each other.

When Children Resist Therapy

Whatever happens in therapy can help me to find out about a child's inner life. Even children who refuse to do anything during sessions, using therapy as yet another arena in which to fight the ongoing battles of their lives, are revealing something. After all, isn't the child playing out something in my room that prevents her from participating in life's opportunities in general?

When one boy came to sessions in my office armed with his homework—which he had clearly counted on as a pursuit guaranteed to command a grown-up's respect—I knew that this was just his way of avoiding any more personal contact with me. This was not so different from his spending recess alone, watching other children from the sidelines.

Another boy, five-year-old Michael, was so fearful of relationships with anyone other than his parents, he couldn't last alone in the room with me for very long. Although he told his mother he wanted to come to see me because he had worries, each time he was in my office he said he wanted to go home. Finally I asked him, "Can you stay if I let you be the boss of how close I get? If I stay in this chair as long as you need me to be here, will it be easier for you?" This lasted one and a half years, but even before we got to the point where I could move around freely, a great deal took place in the room. Aside from his progress in handling his fears about relationships, he shared many terrifying thoughts with me as I remained safely in my chair.

Therapy is probably one of the few places in children's lives where they can adjust slowly, at their own pace, without demands or pressures. These examples show that, even if your child seems to be doing nothing in therapy, you needn't feel that therapy hasn't begun. It begins from the moment she walks through the door, whether she comes in smiling or crying, and whether she talks with the therapist or avoids her entirely.

Tantrums and Therapy

I once treated a child who raged about anything she was expected to do with her family. Before her first play session, her mother called me, very concerned, and said, "She's screaming and yelling, and she's been crying for an hour about coming."

I said, "Fine, that's how she says hello. Now we're beginning. After all, that's what she's here for."

You shouldn't feel that your child has to be good in therapy. If he has behavior problems, you might be so used to worrying about him screaming or breaking things while he's on a play date, or in the supermarket, that you mistakenly transfer those feelings to his behavior in the therapy room. But in fact it's much harder to help a child who feels he has to censor his behavior in my presence. The point is, I want children to show me what the problem is.

Let me tell you more about David, who for so long kept himself from having any outbursts in my presence. Why did I want him to bring his rages to me? I knew he was having tantrums all the time at home and at school, but I didn't know what set him off, and I didn't know how he could be calmed, how he could be helped to restore self-control.

When David finally felt comfortable enough to bring me his rages, I learned a lot. First, he showed me how his anger resulted from assaults to his self-esteem, and his rages were a little boy's way of feeling strong again. I found that helping him feel good about himself in a constructive way, like teaching him how to call

his father, not only distracted him from his tantrum but also left
him with a better feeling about himself when the tantrum had
passed. Mastery is a powerful self-esteem booster, while tantrums perpetuate feelings of being bad.

The day David returned to my office after his summer
vacation, he entered announcing, "I'm going to break your office
apart." He was clearly frightened, but when I asked him what
was troubling him, he just screamed, "I hate it! I don't want to
come back. I'm going to break all your toys!" I knew David was
frightened by the warm feelings he had in seeing me after a long
break; he couldn't stand to know that he was attached. Related
to this awareness, he may have had angry feelings about my
going away for so long.

I was calm and relaxed. I held David in a little wooden chair
with the back of the chair against my knees, and I held his arms
tightly from behind while he tried to bite and kick. He couldn't
do anything harmful. I was able to quietly say all the things
needed to calm him down, to integrate him—basically, "It's
okay, I'm going to help you through it. Let's find another way
for you to tell me what feels so bad. I'll help you stop. You're
having trouble stopping, but I'll help you."

Children are frightened by their own tantrums; they're out
of control, and they know it. If they're allowed to break things
or lash out, or hurt themselves, they become even more frightened by what they're doing, and feel even worse about themselves. By containing David, by letting him know in the calmest
way that I was in control, that I could help him calm down, that I
understood, I began to integrate him.

When I finally felt David's body relax a little, after about
ten minutes, I released him and watched his coping mechanisms
build in a most fascinating way. First, he told me verbally what
he was going to destroy; he'd gone from trying to do it to just
talking about it. Here was a higher form of coping, and I jumped
in to reinforce it. Every time he said he was going to break

something, I'd gasp, "Oh no! My *whole room*!" I denied him the power of actually doing it, but reinforced doing it in fantasy.

As David started saying hostile things to me, without talking about destroying anything, I continued to move him from the power of aggressive acts to the power of word and fantasy. He showed me two new curse signs he had learned in school, and I showed him how impressed I was: "You know *that* curse already!" He started to tell me how he was better at things than I was—how I was such a dummy because I couldn't speak French and he could. I said, "I wish I could speak French! You're so good at that!" He started to feel really good about himself. I watched him, step by step, rise up the developmental ladder, as he tested me on things I didn't know.

By the end of the session, when David went to the toys, he was able to tell me symbolically how much better he felt. He was the good guys, I was the bad guys, and his guys defeated me in a very contained game. He had altogether given up the idea of breaking toys in my office.

Setting Limits. This story introduces another point about oppositional children in therapy—the question of setting limits. When I'm guiding parents whose children act out provocatively or oppositionally, I always advise them to be firm at home. These children need many clear and consistent limits because, however much they try to feel safe by making things go their way, they need the true safety of an adult being in charge.

In therapy, however, I have to try and create a unique, far more permissive atmosphere in which children can feel free to reveal themselves. I do this first by remaining neutral and nonjudgmental, accepting the child for who she is. If she curses, I don't disapprove or act shocked; I let her know that I'm interested in finding out why she's feeling this way. If she kicks or tries to break things, I help her stop, but my emphasis is still on understanding the meaning of her behavior.

Some therapists try to avoid setting limits in the therapy room altogether, aside from the basic rule that children are not allowed to do anything that will hurt themselves or anybody else. I feel, however, that certain actions—such as breaking toys or furniture, or writing on the walls—have to be off limits in therapy just as they are in life. A child like David doesn't feel any better when he's allowed to destroy things; in fact, doing so only makes him feel more bad and unlovable and out of control, because he knows he's not supposed to.

HOW THE PLAY THERAPIST
HOPES TO HELP THE CHILD

Not all children are as frightened to reveal themselves as David. Some will happily sit and talk about their lives for much of a session; others need a little help getting chatting. I find that many of these children have been carrying some real worries around with them, and just offering them a sympathetic ear can often help them on the simplest level.

A small child once told me, "I can't tell this to my mother because she gets so worried when things aren't right." Because the therapist is outside the family situation, children often find it easier to talk to me than they do to those who are close to them. The children also know that it's a therapist's job to keep their secrets, and if they mistrust me at first, I work hard to understand the mistrust and to gain the trust.

As a parent, it can be hard to accept that your child can tell a relative stranger things that he can't tell you, especially if those things are deeply felt. Yet every adult knows how comforting it can be to speak with an attentive and sympathetic person who's not immediately involved, and the same goes for children. They need to get things off their chests.

There are many things your child might want to talk about, but which she dares not mention to you because she thinks you'll get angry or anxious. Perhaps it's nothing much, but it seems very serious to her. Kids can carry all sorts of weighty worries around with them about things they shouldn't have done, things they shouldn't be feeling, or things that are happening in their families, and quite often those worries turn out to be not so serious after all. When the worries are serious, talking about them not only lifts some of the weight, it is also a first step in dealing with them.

Children confide in me about their parents and how they feel about them. One seven-year-old boy whom I saw in consultation was very upset about how much his parents were fighting, because he knew the fights had something to do with him. But he couldn't talk to them about it; he communicated his upset, instead, by regularly soiling his pants. Other children tell me about being bad in school, knowing that they won't get punished; or about how awful their little sister is, knowing that, unlike their parents, I'm not committed to loving both children equally.

Listening. There is a way of listening to children who are having trouble talking about things that are worrying them. First of all, an atmosphere of trust is essential; this is why it's so important for children to have a real sense that what goes on in my room is a secret between us. Confidentiality is my promise to the child, and it can't be broken (although sometimes, if a child agrees, I might invite a parent in to work with us).

Children also have to trust that I won't judge, criticize, punish, or laugh at them, whatever they want to tell me. I have to let them see that I'm calm and interested, and taking in the things he's telling me without undue prompting, or questioning, or asking for more.

Listening to a child's problems can help in a limited way, if he is ready to talk. But for most children this isn't enough. And since quite often children don't really understand what they're feeling, or what it is that's upsetting them, play therapy has to offer a lot more than a sympathetic ear.

Children who are emotionally troubled are usually stuck and need help in some specific areas. Before I talk about these areas individually, let's take another look at Stephanie, the child whom we first met in chapter 1. Even though Stephanie was a child who tended to talk more than play, this little girl's treatment is a wonderful illustration of how children get stuck and how I try to help them. It also shows how, quite often, play therapy deals not with isolated issues but with a whole web of interrelated difficulties that a child brings to treatment.

You probably remember how Stephanie—shy and retiring in school but bossy at home—was trying to control the activities of her famliy as a way of avoiding fearful situations and compensating for feeling so weak outside of her home. The only way she could find to feel better about herself was by feeling she was on top, but in this she paid a price in self-esteem, because she knew her behavior was making her less likable—she was only six, but she was smart enough to know that people don't like bossy children.

Stephanie was trying to cope with her sense of inferiority in a way that backfired, but it was the only thing she knew how to do. Not only did her self-doubts increase, but by behaving in this way she also denied herself the comfort of being protected. Children who feel they run the show can't feel the safety and protection of being contained by the world of grown-ups.

My job, therefore, was to help her in a few major areas. I had to help her understand these feelings; to develop new ways of coping with them; to find new and less bossy ways of relating to people; and to experience herself in a more positive way as someone who could master situations, rather than avoid and resist them.

When she first started in therapy, Stephanie resisted me in little ways. But after about a month she felt comfortable enough to deal with her fears of this new situation by trying to control it, as she had tried to control her family. She would point with an air of absolute authority and tell me, "You're going to get me that game," "You're going to stand up," "Sit down," and so on until, when it was clear that I was not going to comply un-questioningly with her orders, she became completely dis-traught. On the verge of tears, she told me, "This is a terrible place and I'm never coming back!"

"Stephanie," I said, "this is so disappointing for you, isn't it? You thought that this was a place where you could boss a grown-up around, and now you're disappointed." At this point, all I did was to empathize with her despair. She wasn't ready to learn new coping mechanisms yet. She was so sad, and I felt it was too soon to talk about how she was trying to make herself feel better by bossing people around.

When Stephanie was calmer, I helped her to make the first connection—how she was trying to feel safe in this new place by deciding just how things should be. By doing this, I established myself as a person who was interested in learning about her in a noncritical way, and I also laid the groundwork for examining her style of coping with her anxieties.

Stephanie's sense of herself as weak could not be separated from her shaky self-esteem. By avoiding fear-inducing situa-tions, she was preventing herself from developing her sense of being an effective person, able to handle life's challenges, even small ones. This is true of all people who cope by avoiding.

I knew that I would have to work on building Stephanie's self-esteem. But before I could do that, I had to help her un-derstand, in a way that wasn't overwhelming, how badly she felt about herself. Of course, all her behavior had been aimed at covering up those painful feelings. She was still too weak to acknowledge them, and I had to wait until she trusted me be-fore I could help her uncover them without causing her too much pain.

Soon enough, Stephanie found her own way of talking with me about her bad feelings. When she was comfortable with me, and clearly liked me, she began to talk about her friend Kate. As I mentioned earlier, children often use the third person as a way of talking about things that they can't quite own up to—for Stephanie, the third person was a real friend who had problems like her own. Kate became her vehicle for discussing a part of her personality that was too painful to accept as her own. Stephanie was trying to fool me, and she was also trying to fool herself, but she was succeeding in neither.

We went along with these conversations for quite a while, partners in trying to figure out why Kate had these feelings. While Stephanie could discuss Kate's problems quite openly, she could still not accept them as her own. On the contrary, to bolster herself she often told me that all the kids in her class really liked her. She'd say, "Three boys want to marry me," and "All the girls want to be my friend," and then she would tell me how Kate felt that nobody liked her.

So we continued talking about Kate until one day, when it had become clear to me that Stephanie was functioning a little better in her life (partly because her parents were now demanding it) and felt good enough about herself to tolerate some direct exploration of her self-doubts, I finally suggested to her, "You know, I think sometimes *you* have feelings like that."

I waited. Stephanie was quiet for a moment, and then she said yes, maybe she felt a little like that sometimes, but her problems were nowhere near as bad as Kate's. I agreed with her, and then we began to talk about how *she* could feel better about herself. In this way we passed to a new phase of treatment in which Stephanie acknowledged her feelings and was able to move on to a deeper understanding of them. We could now also work on finding new ways for her to cope with situations that made her anxious.

Everything was going well with Stephanie. Her feelings were still painful, but she understood them now, and her self-esteem was improving, so that she no longer had to bolster herself up so much. The improvements showed at home. Stephanie willingly went off to day camp and accompanied her parents on social outings, and the battles were far less frequent, which also helped her to feel better about herself.

One day Stephanie's parents came for their conference and mentioned that Stephanie was having some trouble relating to her friends in her new class at school. They also told me that she'd been having trouble sleeping at night recently.

Children always know that I see their parents, and if something important comes up, I'll usually mention it to the child. So when Stephanie came for her next session, I told her, "Your mom and dad were here, and they told me there's something on your mind I might be able to help you with."

She was so relieved to speak about her new dilemma. She told me that she didn't want to be a selfish girl whom the other kids would hate, yet she knew she was weak and didn't want to be taken advantage of. After we had explored what each of these positions meant to her, and what kind of child she wanted to be, I could offer her very concrete advice on dealing with this problem.

We worked together on how a girl can know if what she wants is selfish, and how, if it isn't, she can hold her position firmly. I also helped her to understand the link between her struggles around being in a new class in school and the fact that she was having trouble sleeping.

I said, "You may wonder how come you're having trouble falling asleep even though everything's the same at home as usual, but you know what? Sometimes when you're working very hard on something in your life, like figuring out how to make friends, you can come home and not be able to stop working on the problem, and so you can't get to sleep. What a surprise! Because the big work's being done at school during the day, and the problem's at home at bedtime! But they really can be connected."

It's unusual for children to have problems in only one area. If a child can't control his impulses, that will be reflected in his sense of himself as a bad person. If a child secretly believes that he has caused his parents' divorce, his guilt is likely to lead him to some misguided behaviors designed to help him deny these feelings to himself. But if he can be helped to understand what he's feeling and why, he can begin to feel and act differently.

Helping Children to Understand Themselves

Like Stephanie, who had to be guided toward an understanding of why she acted the way she did, children do not have the self-awareness to understand many of the links between the way they feel, why they feel it, and what that feeling makes them do. No matter how many times you ask your young child in exasperation, "Why do you have to hit another kid every time they won't let you play?" he can't answer, because he doesn't yet have the intellectual wherewithal to draw to such psychological connections. One of the benefits of therapy is that it helps a child develop the capacity to make these kinds of links.

A child might know what sets him off. He might recognize a pattern in the fact that every time another kid excludes him, he has to punch him in the face. But he's not able to understand why—how, for instance, his response might be fueled by feelings he's been having at home.

Children have a particularly hard time linking events that happen in two different places; that's why I had to ease Stephanie's anxieties about not being able to get to sleep at home, by drawing the connection with her feelings about being in a new class at school. By helping her to understand, I defused her worries about sleep, and soon the sleep problem disappeared.

When a child verbalizes his anxieties, it's not hard for an adult to help him make these kinds of connections. But when he can't or won't put his feelings into words, they often emerge through play, just as Mary's feelings about her family emerged when she created doll families without children. Once revealed, the next step was to begin helping her put her feelings into words that she could understand. "Mary," I observed when I thought she was ready to look at her communication, "there's no room for children in this family!" I didn't make any reference to her specifically; I'll often keep the interpretation general by saying "a child" or "that doll," so that children don't feel confronted by what I'm suggesting.

Mary didn't say anything. She went on playing, but I knew that she had heard and understood. Putting her feelings into words served several functions. First, I was now able to show her that her anger had a reason—she wasn't just a bad child, as she had come to see herself. Her feelings, now verbalized for her, could become part of her self-awareness—an easily stored and easily retrievable package that was hers to examine, to contemplate, and to understand herself through. In the following weeks we worked on figuring out what Mary really wanted and how she could show her parents that she was upset, without being so angry in her behavior.

I was also able to use the insight I gained through Mary's play to help her parents become aware of how Mary, rather than being just oppositional, was angry about something real in the family setup, so that instead of battling in general they could try to work things out around the issue that was upsetting their daughter. (I'll talk more about this in chapter 4, "Parent-Work.")

It's always very important for parents to share in and adjust to the new perceptions that are a part of my work in helping children to become more self-aware. Obviously, if your child is beginning to see herself as "a gooder girl" than she thought she was, or more capable, the way you relate to her, and what you expect of her, has to reflect that. My work with Jack, the phobic boy whom I mentioned earlier, is a good illustration.

One of Jack's major obstacles as he entered treatment was homework. Of course, many children have trouble sitting down to homework, but for Jack and his family it had become a nightmare. He would get very frightened over it every night, screaming and yelling, "I can't do it!" Getting through the homework, even a little bit of it, took forever, and by the time he got to bed very late every night, the whole family was exhausted by the drama of Jack's homework.

So I had Jack bring his homework into my office; I wanted to see what the trouble was, what was making him so anxious, and possibly, how to handle the job. First of all, we did the work together. I could see how he panicked the minute something began to frustrate him. He didn't scream and yell as he did at home, because he didn't know me well enough yet, but he withdrew from the slightest challenge.

I had to focus Jack on his work so that he could see that he *could* do it. It was easier for me than for his parents, because, as I said, he didn't know me well enough yet to regress completely into a screaming state. While reassuring him, I helped him structure his working process into little doses that he could tolerate; I wouldn't let him move away from the table until he had finished copying a written line or completed a math problem. As he progressed, we expanded the doses, and Jack's image of himself as a boy who couldn't manage the work began to change.

Through this process I helped Jack learn about himself. I wanted him to understand what he did in the face of a challenge, and so I pointed out to him how it wasn't that he couldn't do the work (he was really a smart boy), but that as soon as it got a little difficult, he did something that made it impossible to carry on—he became frightened and ran away from it. I told him, "You're so worried that you won't be able to do something, that you never find out if you can."

When things had become a little easier, I called Jack's mother in. I wanted her to watch how I worked with Jack so that she could do the same, first by working in my office with him while I watched, and later at home. But mainly, I wanted her to see that he could do the work, so that she would demand more, and I wanted Jack to know that she knew he could do it, because her perception and expectations of him had such an important effect on his self-image.

Helping the Child to Find New Ways of Coping

Before Jack began treatment with me, his parents were quite unable to explain his fears and phobias around issues such as homework or going upstairs by himself. As I learned more about him, I was able to show his parents how Jack's totally incomprehensible and difficult behavior was in fact his unsuccessful attempt to cope with something that troubled him. He was an avoider, but avoiding difficult things did nothing to ease his anxieties.

Jack wasn't unusual in this; many children evolve maladaptive styles of coping with life's difficulties. The little girl who is scared that none of her classmates like her might try to stave off rejection by angrily pushing them away first: "I don't like you! I don't want to play with you!" Of course, coping mechanisms like these can only make the matter worse. My job is to teach children practical and effective ways of coping with their feelings, or with situations that make them anxious, so that they can function in their worlds and begin to feel better about themselves. The two often go hand in hand.

In helping Jack to figure out a way that he could sit down and ride out his feelings of anxiety over challenging homework, I encouraged him to find a new way of coping other than avoidance. At the same time, it was important for Jack to understand why he tended to react in such negative ways. In helping children to find new ways of coping, I work with them to slowly explore the reasons for their feelings.

One five-year-old patient of mine, the impulsive Betty, shouted "I hate you!" whenever she felt most warmly toward me;

she was compelled to fight against feelings of attachment to another person, because she was afraid of being disappointed. These feelings spilled over into every area of her life, wherever other people were involved. It also affected her life in that, by having to stay strong and adversarial, she couldn't accept compliments or offers of help, and had trouble being close to all but a few select people.

In the beginning I showed Betty how she could cope with her anxiety without provoking me, by keeping a safe but friendly distance from me. Then, as her fears eased, every time Betty reverted to acting belligerently, I would tell her gently, "Oh, you like to trick me and hide your secret good feelings." Several months later, this little exchange had become our private joke.

Effective coping has to have a rational basis. An intensely shy child, for instance, might respond impulsively to a room full of strange children by running away. My job is to teach him how to cope with his shyness through rituals that can get him through the situations he finds so difficult; for instance, by counting to five, walking into the room, focusing on one child, going over and saying hello. Rituals like these can serve children for life. I might teach another child how to cope with anger, not through physical outbursts, but by working things out through a teacher or parent.

The point is to steer children toward a thinking mode, rather than a screaming or fleeing mode, in the way they cope with their feelings. Jack's case provides a good example. He would often come to my office, bringing his rages with him all the way from school. In one instance, he was upset because he hadn't been given the part he wanted in a school play. He came in totally out of control, screaming the whole story at me, his anger spilling over to me although he was unaware of that. Nothing I said made any difference. He just yelled, "I don't want to hear that!" or "I know that!" So I became very quiet, and then he started screaming, "Don't be so silent!"

"Jack," I told him, "everything I say seems to feel wrong to you. Do you want me to continue talking?"

Little by little he calmed down, and we started to talk a little bit. I asked him, "Are you upset because you wanted to be in the play, or because you feel rejected?" Everything I said to him was designed to help him regain his rational self. He told me he wanted to be in the play. I pointed out to him that maybe someone else had the right face for the part, or maybe it was someone else's turn, and he said, "Well, I was the best." I agreed that he would make a very good actor, and I said, "Well, let's see, you didn't get this role. What else can a boy do?"

I insisted that he think with me, using his mind instead of his raw emotions to cope with his upset. We talked about how else he might get to perform, and when he was able to be calm and thoughtful, we explored the basis for his pain. By the time he left my office, Jack was calm, reintegrated, and functioning on a far more rational level.

Learning New Ways of Relating to People

Children start developing ways of relating to other people from birth. The child acts a certain way, her parents act a certain way, and they all interact in a certain way. The experiences of the baby in her relationships with her parents are repeated over and over again, and so fixed patterns of relating are quickly formed.

With these fixed patterns come expectations. As the baby grows, he comes to anticipate that this is what people are like, and therefore this is what it feels like to be in the world of people. The child's way of behaving around other people is shaped by these expectations. If he only manages to get his needs met when he screams, he will soon learn to scream when he needs something, whoever he is with. If he always get cuddled when he acts his most babylike, he will use infantile behavior to gain affection from the people around him.

Some children learn never to ask for anything, because they anticipate being disappointed. One girl I was treating was always there for her friends and very interested in helping others. To some extent this was her only way of relating, because she couldn't take on the other role—she could not expect her friends to have anything to give her. Others learn that the only way they can get their parents' attention is by getting into trouble or crying. Many of the children I see, who live in busy, two-career families, have learned that it's the squeaky wheel that gets the oil.

When a child has relationship problems, it doesn't mean that he doesn't treat other people nicely; it means that there's something that goes on between the child and other people that we need to work on. When Betty, the little girl with the secret good feelings, started treatment at four and a half, she could only feel safe in a relationship if she was opposing the other person. That was what we needed to work on.

By controlling her interactions with others, Betty felt less vulnerable in their hands. It was almost as if she were fighting for her life, whatever the cost. At home, Betty would forego special treats rather than submit to her mother and wait until after dinner. She rejected any kind of compliment or positive feedback because she *had* to take the opposing position. If someone said, "You really did that job well," she'd say, "No I didn't," although she hungrily craved the recognition. But the biggest price Betty paid was in her resistance to seeing herself as part of a warm and loving relationship. She denied herself that comfort as a child, and I knew that in the future, as she grew up, she would have weak models on which to base warm and loving adult relationships, in spite of having adoring parents.

Children like Betty, whose problems are relational, often find it easier to break out of their patterns in a new place, with a new person. Therapy offers them this fresh environment, and in establishing myself as a nonjudgmental, interested person, it's easier for me than for a parent to point out to these children the meaning or negative consequences of their behavior, without their feeling criticized (a hard balance to strike, as any parent of a school-aged child must know).

In working with Betty and children like her, I generally concentrate on the relationship we build in the therapy room. New coping techniques, as I mentioned earlier, are stopgap measures that help the child to be in the room with me while we become familiar with each other. When I work on relationship problems, I have to start with a certain closeness and trust; then I can start to move things along and help the child to see people differently. Because I respond to the child's provocations in an unexpected way—by not getting upset or angry—anticipations begin to break down.

Every little exchange that happens in the room serves as a way of exploring the relationship, and through it other relationships. One day, Betty crawled into my lap and said, in reference to the therapist in the neighboring office, "I like Naomi better than you." I knew this wasn't a literal statement; she hardly knew Naomi, and she was evidently very attached to me by this point. What she was doing was trying to create a rivalry between Naomi and me, just like the rivalry between her divorced parents.

I said, "You know, you could like us both, even though you feel you have to choose who you like better. You don't have to choose who you like better with your parents either, even though they're divorced."

Betty crawled even deeper into my lap and said, "I'm going to kill you!"

I said, "Kill me with love I bet!" And she giggled; she didn't push it away.

In that little exchange so much was touched upon—our relationship, her ability to live out other relationships through ours, her relationships with her parents, her desire to love and be loved.

Sorting Out Confused Beliefs

Four-year-old Mark came into my office one day and announced, "All the kids in my school have to be friends, so I can be as mean as I want and I'll still have friends."

Every parent knows how children tend to put two and two together and make five. Sometimes the notions they come up with are quite amusing, but sometimes they're the cause of considerable trouble. Children in treatment with me are often troubled by worrisome or confused beliefs such as, "If I let someone get close, I'll get hurt," or "If I grow up too much, I'll lose the protection and comfort of my parents."

Sara, for instance, was almost four when she first came to me for treatment, and was still too fearful of losing the warmth and pretection of babyhood to allow herself to give up the bottle or be fully toilet trained. Playing in my office one day, Sara took a baby kangaroo out of the mother kangaroo's pouch and began to move the baby away from the mother. Suddenly she stopped, turned to me anxiously, and said, "Oh! Oh! She'd better get right back inside that pouch so her mommy can take care of her."

"Sara, " I said, "even if the baby moves away from the pouch, her mommy will still take good care of her."

Sara looked at me in surprise; this was an entirely new idea for her. I repeated it several times, and then I said, "You know, we have an expert right outside in the waiting room who knows everything there is to know about being a mommy. Shall I call her in?"

I felt that Sara needed her mother's confirmation on this important point, so I invited her into the room and told her that we'd asked her to join us because she knew so much about being a mother. "Tell us," I said, "when the baby kangaroo leaves the mother's pouch, will the mother still take good care of her?"

Sara's mother smiled and said, "Of course, always."

"There," I told Sara. "And she knows all about being a mother."

Sara looked up with a big smile. "And *I* know all about being a child!"

Because of the way a young child reasons, he can easily jump to false conclusions about emotional issues, linking barely related factors—like the fact that his grandmother just got sick and that a little while ago he was mad at her for being so strict—into cause and effect: "My grandmother got sick because I wished she'd go away," or "My parents are fighting because I was bad and hit the baby."

Because children are by nature egocentric in their thinking, this kind of confused self-blame is fairly common. When important things happen in their worlds for no clear reason, they have to find a way of placing themselves at the center. If Mommy is in an especially good mood one day, it's because of the beautiful picture he drew for her; but if things go wrong in the family, he has to search his memory for his own past naughtinesses that will explain why.

Small children have such a very limited experience and understanding of the world around them—the passage of time, death, growth, love, to say nothing of bank balances and job troubles—that it should come as no surprise to you when you discover the kinds of confused notions your child has been troubled with. Yet it's often hard for parents to guess at the illogical beliefs their children have formed, because grown-ups just don't think that way.

A three-year-old, for example, might decide that her parents don't love her anymore and are going to abandon her, because if they did love her, they'd send the new baby back to where it came from. But because she's only three, she can't express her anxiety directly, and nobody can figure out why she's constantly and desperately clinging to her mother.

I often discover and address these kinds of beliefs through a child's play, as I did with Sara. Sometimes an incidental comment a child makes while we're talking will reveal his confused thinking. I have learned to listen for it, both in play and in talk.

One little boy, Sam, who was resisting being potty trained, happened to mention to me that he disliked birthday cake because he didn't like messes and neither did his mother. The connection between messes and toilet training was obvious, but his mother, who was in the room, said she had no problem with the idea of messy cake and smeared faces. However, she realized that Sam had picked up on the fact that she didn't like what she called "emotional messes" in her life and what he probably perceived as her need to have everything just so and in control. Once we understood Sam's distorted logic, it wasn't hard for his mother and me to help him to see things differently.

DEVELOPING SELF-ESTEEM

It's very hard to have problems in your life and not have them affect your sense of self-worth. Nearly every child introduced in this book suffers from self-esteem problems tied into other difficulties.

Betty couldn't feel very good about herself, because she related to people so oppositionally that they often got angry with her; David felt terrible about himself, and the tough-guy stance he adopted to compensate didn't endear him to anybody, which only made him feel more unlovable; Jack felt weak, and his panics made him worry about being "crazy," as he put it to me; even little Sara wistfully told me that no one her age still drank from bottles; and Stephanie's bossy-timid dual persona made her feel very unlikable.

Without an adequate sense of self-worth, it's very hard for any child to take the necessary risks or accept the inevitable disappointments of growing up. Yet parents don't always recognize self-esteem problems because children, in their efforts to get back to a tolerable sense of self, so often compensate by acting tough.

Mark, you may remember, used to tyrannize his family

constantly by insisting, for instance, that "the walls are black"; asserting himself and controlling people in this way made him feel strong. He would fly into a rage if anyone argued with him, and wouldn't give up until they agreed.

I figured out very quickly that if I could allow Mark to save face, I didn't have to go along with any of his tyrannical games. So when he pointed and said, "That book's blue," when in fact it was red, I would laugh and say, "You're the funniest kid I know. You love to trick grown-ups!" Of course, being the funniest kid and tricking grown-ups made him feel really powerful, and he was able to give up the game with his sense of self in tact. Once his attempts at self-esteem bolstering were understood, both his parents and I could help work on the underlying problem.

How Self-Esteem Is Built Naturally in the Course of Therapy

As I help children to deal more successfully with their feelings, conflicts, and the demands of daily life, they begin to experience themselves more positively.

The child who is driven by feelings of jealously and resentment feels like a bad person. Her powerful emotions—which she can't understand, let alone come to terms with—make her wet the bed or attack other children in school. Of course, this kind of behavior tends to make people angry at her, which makes her feel even worse about herself. But if she can understand that she's angry and scared because Mommy and Daddy are fighting, then she feels a huge relief, and maybe the bed-wetting stops, Mommy doesn't get so angry, and she begins to feel like a better person.

Practical Ways of Building Self-Esteem

Quite often I help children develop a stronger sense of self by working with them in a more practical way, helping them to develop coping mechanisms for dealing with social and emotional challenges, as I did with Stephanie in the latter part of her treatment when we talked about how to make friends.

I also worked with her on another level, helping her to remember all the things she could do well. I'd say, "It's so hard for you to remember all the things you're good at when you get stuck on one thing you can't do," thereby giving her a mechanism for sustaining her sense of self-worth.

When I work with children on self-esteem, I'll pick up on things that they do in the room or bring in that show a real effort. It's a way of helping the child define himself in a positive way. I might say, "You worked very hard on this picture and got it to look the way you wanted." This then becomes a part of the child's developing awareness of his strengths and weaknesses, based on real evidence.

Perhaps most important of all, I work on mastery as the key to self-esteem. As Jack learned to master his fears, he found that he felt strong enough to do things he used to avoid. He could go to the pool, because he no longer dreaded the taunts of some of the other boys; he had answers ready for them and, in fact, because Jack was less fearful, the other boys accepted him more readily. A child who is a doer is inevitably going to have more confidence than an avoider, and of course that confidence affects how others see her, as well as how she sees herself. That's why I encourage parents to expect the most that's reasonable from their children, rather than indulge them in their reticence.

I work very hard with parents in this area, asking them to make certain demands on children that are within their capabilities. Stephanie's parents began to demand more of her in the sense of meeting the challenge of new situations, like a new after-school class. Jack's parents expected him to do his homework; it had to be in small doses, but those doses grew progressively bigger as Jack's ability to tolerate the stress increased. There has to be a challenge involved, because if you don't ask a child to stretch herself, she'll never develop a sense of her capacity to master things.

Concrete Skills. As I've already said, learning new concrete skills helps many children to develop more confidence in themselves. When Mark insisted that there were two checkers on the board when in fact there were four, I taught him to count by touch—one, two, three, four—and he immediately let go of the contest. Now that he knew how to count just like a grown-up, he felt good enough for the time being not to need the power struggle that his game represented.

The concrete skills learned through play can help a child to feel stronger. David, who you probably remember couldn't stand to lose at games, and used to play Connect Four with me at each session, cheated frantically to make sure he won. But as his expertise increased to the point where he was able to win in a fair game, I told him, "I think you really do know now that you're a good Connect Four player, so even when you lose, you can still remember you're a good player because you've won so often." At this point, David could safely play board games with other children. His experience of himself as someone who often won was strong enough to sustain him in the event of a loss.

Self-Esteem and the Learning-Disabled Child

Learning-disabled children are especially vulnerable to self-esteem problems. Since school is the place where their abilities are measured and compared on a daily basis, these children suffer constant blows to their sense of worth. Even though a child is bright and has an excellent grasp of math, his problems around reading can easily make him feel like a "dummy."

Many of the things I do in helping learning-disabled children build a stronger self-esteem are in essence the same as my self-esteem work with other children: helping them to understand the areas in which their strengths lie, whether it's in math or in drawing or in the imaginative power of storytelling, and helping them stretch themselves so that they can see that learning is not impossible, just difficult.

One of the first things I often do is to define the meaning of "learning disabled" in terms that a child can understand. Many children will accept this definition from an "expert" more readily than from another adult. It's very reassuring for a child to come to understand that learning disabled doesn't mean stupid. It means the surprising presence of impaired learning in one or more areas in someone who otherwise demonstrates a much higher intelligence than their work in those areas would suggest—in other words, "What a surprise that someone as smart as you are in so many ways is having trouble with math!"

I might also tell an older child, "You know, right now it seems as if school's your whole life and it feels a bit overwhelming to have this problem, but at some point you're going to find a job that's going to use your strengths and then you'll feel good about yourself. But you've got to get through school first." This is where learning specialists or tutors take over.

Michael, the boy who had me sit in the chair while he played, was learning disabled. I used to have him bring in his report cards and we'd go through them together, talking about what he was good at, what he wasn't good at. He had problems with writing, and I told him, "I know someone who's very successful in his profession, and he's learning disabled like you are. He uses a typewriter. Someday you'll use a typewriter, too."

I also spoke with Michael's teacher and asked that, since he had trouble with the written word, perhaps as a way of compensating she could give him a little extra time standing in front of the class talking; despite his learning problems, Michael was extremely articulate with the spoken word, allowing his superior intelligence to show through.

It helped Michael just to be able to bring in his anxieties and talk about them. He was always in fear of the next assignment, the next grade. He needed reassurance—not empty compliments or unreasonable expectations, but a realistic and supportive environment in which he could explore his feelings and sort out who he really was: a smart boy who had a little more to deal with in his life than some.

4
꧁꧂

PARENT-WORK

Finally, you have your child settled into treatment with a therapist of your choice. It wasn't easy. From the time you first started to have doubts about your child's emotional well-being, you worried, you discussed it with friends and professionals, you turned it over and over in your mind.

Then you began to seek out a therapist. You sought referrals, made phone calls, interviewed prospective child therapists, introduced your child to the idea, brought her for consultation, dealt with her anxieties and your own, and reassured her about her first session. And finally, you think to yourself, all that hard work is over.

In fact, your work as a parent of a child in therapy is far from over, because from the moment your child enters therapy, and play therapy in particular, you make a commitment to carry out your end of a three-way arrangement among the therapist, the child, and yourselves. Without such a commitment, you are only giving therapy half a chance to help your child. As you read this chapter, you'll understand why I consider parent-work to be so important a part of child treatment, and why I strongly recommend that you make sure at the outset of your child's treatment that the therapist is available to work with you, to listen to what you have to tell her about your child's life at home, and to help you refine your style of parenting so that it matches what your child needs.

WHAT IS PARENT-WORK?

When Jack's parents, Mr. and Mrs. Simpson, first came to see me, I told them that I would need to schedule regular parent meetings with them, and tried to help them understand why the collaborative working relationship between therapist and parents would be so important to their child's treatment.

Home, I explained, is the most important part of a child's world, and parents are the most important people in it. I pointed out to them that, as a parent, you are a central figure in your child's treatment for many reasons. Firstly, you can help to connect the various aspects of your child's life—primarily home, school, and the therapist's office. Secondly, a major aspect of my role as a therapist is to offer guidance on practical parenting problems, and so to help you help your child. And thirdly, since your feelings about yourself as a parent are bound to influence your relationship with your child, it's often helpful to explore these feelings with someone who can help you to understand and come to terms with them. That, too, is my job as a child therapist.

During the next several months, I worked with Mr. and Mrs. Simpson. We helped one another, all three of us focusing on Jack's problems. His parents filled me in on what was happening at home and at school, and I let them know how things were going in Jack's treatment. I also helped them both come to terms with their own feelings about their troubled son—they had been feeling totally helpless, as if nothing was going to work, and they worried about what Jack's future would be like. They were extremely frustrated with Jack for making their day-to-day lives so difficult, while I sensed that they also felt terribly guilty about what they saw as their role in all of this.

As time went on, I helped them feel less desperate, less guilty, less frustrated, and more in control of the situation by showing them that there really was a way to help Jack. I also gave them practical guidance on how they could work with Jack at home, helping him to gain confidence in himself and to stem his panicky outbursts of anger and frustration, in some of the same ways that I was helping him in my office.

Much of my work with parents involves translating what I do with a child in the office into suggestions for parents about things they can do at home. In sessions with Jack's parents I used to basically say, "When Jack is so upset, it's not helpful to soothe him by gratifying him—by telling him you'll get him a toy or go for a treat. When a child is Jack's age, eight or nine, he's too complicated to be soothed like that. He knows it's not a solution, and often ends up feeling angry when it's offered. What does soothe him is to get him functioning at a level where he feels more in control, so if you can engage him in thinking about the problem rather than emotionally flailing over it, he feels much better and it reintegrates him; he feels whole again, like a stronger person."

A great deal of my ongoing work with Mr. and Mrs. Simpson had to do with limit setting and structuring more responsibility for Jack, and with very practical issues such as what to do about after-school activities—Jack insisted he wanted to do them all and yet he kept dropping out of them. I tried to help his parents determine when they should insist that he keep up with an after-school program and when they could let him drop out. For instance, piano lessons required so much practice and time in the life of a boy who had enough trouble getting his homework done, that I felt this was one activity he could give up—there was a real problem there, whereas the swim team, where he felt at a disadvantage because he wasn't the best swimmer and disliked being splashed, really helped him to develop an important skill for life, and helped him to overcome his frailties. I felt it was important to Jack's self-awareness that he develop more of a physical sense of himself, and so suggested to Jack's parents that they strongly encourage him to continue with the swim team.

Jack's mother would always call when Jack was terribly upset about something—first of all to review the way she had handled his feeling upset, and second to look at what she could do to prevent it from happening again—and I would call her when I felt there was something important to convey to her; there was a real interaction in our relationship. Once, for instance, when Jack was eleven, his mother left a message for me that Jack had been sick and off school, but now it was two weeks later and he was still complaining about headaches and still staying home from school. Nobody knew whether he really had felt the headaches or whether he was just malingering. This was a boy, after all, who had trouble going back to school after the weekend, and even more trouble after a vacation—was he just anxious about school now, and consciously or unconsciously exaggerating a slight physical discomfort because of his anxiety?

Before the findings came in, showing that Jack had no medical problem, I called his mother back with the suggestion that if he said he wasn't feeling well, she could let him stay home, but should do nothing to make being at home especially pleasurable for him—no treats, no extra attention, no hovering over him. Two days later Mrs. Simpson called to let me know that she had figured out a plan based on the principle I had given her. She had gone out for the day, leaving Jack with everything he might need, including a number where she could be reached, and had called in periodically to check on him.

The next day Jack was ready for school: The plan had worked, although it was not a permanent cure. This, in my view, is the essence of parent-work. I try to give basic principles, but every family has its own way of doing things, and parents are very creative in the way they shape my suggestions to fit in with their own rituals and routines.

Many other issues were discussed between Jack's parents and myself during parent sessions, but the story so far should give you some idea of the range of parent-work—the communication of information about the child through meetings and phone contact; emotional support and practical guidance for the parents; plans to be carried out at home; and recommendations and referrals to other forms of treatment, or in some cases to special activities that I feel would benefit the child.

Of course, the issues vary depending on the needs of the parents and of the child. But fundamental to this aspect of a child's treatment is the opportunity for parents and therapist to work together in such a way that the therapy a child receives in my office for a couple of hours each week is echoed in the way her life at home is shaped. And the home—its shape and values—is also considered in the way I work with the family.

WHAT FORMS CAN PARENT-WORK TAKE?

As in Jack's case, parent-work usually takes the form of regular parent sessions that complement my sessions with the child. But it's not always so. Before I go on to say more about this form of parent-work, let me tell you about some other forms it can take.

Depending on my assessment of a child's needs, and of the parents', I might occasionally recommend parent-work without child treatment, or separate therapy for parents with someone else, along with my treatment of the child. Not all therapists use these options, but it's always worth discussing them if you feel they're appropriate.

Parent-Work Without Child Treatment

A mother called me one day about her little girl, Rebecca, who had suddenly started having severe separation problems. She had always been somewhat distressed when it came to separating from home and parents, her mother told me, but one day, while they were staying in their country house, she went out saying that she would be back at a certain time and came back instead a half hour later. After that, Rebecca couldn't be in a room alone. She was always sure her parents were going to abandon her.

Rebecca's mother came for a consultation, and from what she told me, it seemed as if everything else in her daughter's life was going fine. I also saw Rebecca, who seemed immensely relieved just to know that her problem was being addressed, and to be able to tell me about her baby brother and how much she resented him. Clearly, her separation problems had something to do with the idea that her brother had replaced her in her parents' lives. Although she'd been very quiet about it, I could see that she felt as if her parents weren't available to care for her as much as they had been in the past. This was a big problem for Rebecca, because she thought she couldn't handle the tasks that her age demanded of her without the help of a parent. She didn't feel strong enough in herself, although in reality she was quite competent in most ways.

I decided not to treat this girl directly, but rather through parent-work alone. As I've said, her problems seemed well contained in this specific area, and I also felt that this was a family who could really help their child at home. So I worked with her parents, showing them how they needed to build up Rebecca's sense of herself as a strong person by allowing her increasing autonomy—with their support and encouragement to bolster her.

I explained how they could reflect her developing sense back to her, and how it was important for them to never assume that just because she did something new, it was part of her self-image. A child really needs to have his growth confirmed by his parents before that growth can become a part of his self-image—"Look at you! You can do these things!" I also called their attention to the fact that Rebecca felt displaced by the baby. She had always been such a good sister that they had never suspected there was any problem in that area.

Rebecca's case was not altogether unusual. Occasionally, after an initial consultation with parents, I will recommend a form of treatment that involves little or no contact with the child. I frequently do this if I feel that the problem, like Rebecca's, is well contained and doesn't seep into other areas of the child's life, or that the child's problem is primarily temperamental—basically, a matching of parenting styles to the needs of the child. As I did with Rebecca, I work with the parents by offering them guidance on how to deal with the specific issue that has brought them to me.

My format is to meet parents and hear about the problem. I then meet the child, usually (but not always) twice, to get a more complete picture of him, and then I meet once more with the parents to ask further questions and to give them my impressions and recommendations. I always suggest that they let me know how things are going, even through a phone call or a short note. Parents often return for one or more follow-up sessions if they feel they want more guidance, or to revise the suggestions.

Quite often, as the child himself changes in response to new kinds of parenting suggested in parent-work, the way you handle him has to change, too. Rebecca's mother, for instance, called me again a few months after our consultation to tell me that Rebecca had been behaving in a highly oppositional way. She couldn't understand why, or what to do about it.

I had Rebecca come in and I talked to her, and then I met with her mother. I told her, "You've done such a good job, that her separation anxieties have diminished. She's no longer terrified of losing your love, and so now she can let you know how angry she is about certain things." This session focused on how Rebecca's parents, while acknowledging the source of her anger, could set firmer limits for a girl who now felt stronger and more able to tolerate them.

Three months later her mother called to say that things were going fine, and I told her that there was no need to call again unless there was a problem. However, if after some time Rebecca's problems had not diminished, despite my work with her parents, then I would have reconsidered my recommendation of no therapy for Rebecca herself.

Let's talk briefly about the kinds of situations that most often lead me to recommend parent-work without child treatment:

The Difficult Child. I often try parent-work by itself in the case of the "difficult child"—the child who is temperamentally difficult from birth. As I mentioned in chapter 1, the difficult child is not necessarily troubled or in need of help, but problems develop because parents are understandably at a loss for how to handle these children effectively, and are confused about the reasons for their difficult behavior.

Because temperament isn't readily changed or outgrown, parents often need help in learning how to handle their difficult children in order to be able to help them. These children need extra help from their parents in the area of control and in working through the recurrent stumbling blocks of their personalities. If the work starts early enough, it's often possible to avoid difficulties that begin as temperamental spreading to other areas such as self-esteem, which could require direct treatment in child sessions.

Toilet Training and Other Practical Issues. I might also recommend parent contact without child treatment in the case of a child who's having trouble with a specific, practical issue such as toilet training or sleep, but is otherwise doing well. I can offer practical recommendations on how to handle the problem.

I already mentioned, in an earlier chapter, a little girl whose parents consulted me because she had been refusing to sleep in her own bed at night. This child, I felt, didn't need treatment because she was doing well in all other areas of her life, and her family seemed perfectly able to work with her at home, given a little guidance.

I told her parents how to walk the child back to her bed each time, staying with her until she settled in. I told them that even if they had to wake up and leave their own bed all night at first, it would be an investment that would pay off for everyone. The longer you wait, the harder it is to resolve this type of problem, and a child needs to know that he can be safe in his own bed—that's part of growing up.

If I feel, however, that a sleep or toilet-training issue has created or is symptomatic of a larger struggle that will emerge in some other form, then I'll probably recommend therapy for the child, in conjunction with parent-work.

Separate Therapy for Parents

Sometimes parents need a little more help than is available in parent sessions to deal with problems of their own that are contributing to the child's difficulty. Depending on the nature of the problem, I might recommend individual therapy for one parent, couples therapy, or a parent support group if I know of one that's appropriate.

Any time there's real marital tension in the home, it's impossible for the children not to be affected by it. In these cases I always recommend couples therapy, although of course it's up to the parents to decide whether they want to do this or not. After a year of working with David's parents, for example, I suggested to them that they consult with a couples therapist. The children were often pulled into the fights between the parents, and David found himself dragged by his father into competition for his mother's attention. There was so much tension in the home resulting from problems within their marriage, and that tension was undoubtedly impacting on the children.

If a therapist recommends treatment for you, it doesn't mean that you're being blamed. It's just one way of trying to help a child who is feeling the impact of many factors in her daily life. Therapy attempts to touch all the pieces of the child's world that affect her personality.

Quite often there's just one issue that needs to be dealt with more intensively than is possible in the context of a scheduled parents' visit. For example, a very able mother whose daughter I was treating once told me, "You know, when my daughter becomes needy, when she regresses into baby talk or acts in an infantile way, it's intolerable to me, and I know this is wrong."

She was aware that her response was in some way connected with her relationship to her own mother, but she needed extra help in overcoming this blind spot in her relationship with her child. Although the problem seemed specific, she eventually realized that her difficulties in this area even affected her ability to provide certain kinds of support to her husband. Recognizing the broad reach of her conflict, she entered her own therapy to work on it.

Another mother felt accused, and yet overly determined to change, every time I tried to offer her practical guidance. My parenting suggestions seemed to confirm her view of herself as a destroyer of her children. In fact, she was a very good, although anxious mother, but when her children had problems, she blamed herself entirely. I felt that her anxiety about her parenting was being carried over to her children, so I suggested that she consult a therapist of her own about the issue.

Sometimes parents want to take a more careful look at their

feelings about their children. A parent might say, "I know I should love all my children the same, but this child has special meaning to me." In fact, it's common for parents to identify more strongly with one of their children. You may love them all yet feel a stronger bond with the first child, or a better understanding for the child that reminds you of yourself, or a certain impatience with another child. At times it's enough for a parent to share these feelings with someone who can help organize them. But if you feel uncomfortable about your feelings and want to examine them more closely, speak to the therapist about additional therapy for yourself and ask for a referral.

Parent-Work in Conjunction With the Child's Therapy

Most commonly parent-work takes the form of regular parental contact with the therapist in conjunction with the child's treatment. The format varies. Usually there is a regularly scheduled, forty-five-minute to one-hour parent session, which might be every two to six weeks or as often as once a week. Some therapists establish a fixed schedule for meetings, but many, including myself, schedule according to need—generally more frequently near the beginning of treatment or during a period when a great deal is happening in the child's life or in his therapy. Even when there's less regular contact, I maintain phone contact with parents as needed, encouraging them to call me with any concerns or questions, as I call them whenever I feel there's something they need to know.

What Happens During a Typical Parent Session?

Before I go into detail about the kinds of things that are usually dealt with in parent sessions, let me give some idea of how a typical session progresses.

I usually begin a parent meeting by asking parents to follow up on anything we discussed last time or by phone since then. For instance, one child's mother, Mrs. Allen, told me about bedtime. It had been a very serious problem, and since she and her husband realized that at those critical times their son felt comforted by extreme rituals, I had already suggested to Mrs. Allen that she devise some fairly rigid bedtime routines. Mrs. Allen told me that it was working well. She had one question: If her husband took over the bedtime routine one night, could he substitute making up a story, as he liked to do, instead of reading a book? I said that he could certainly try it, as long as he made the connection to his son so that the sequence wouldn't be lost.

After we've talked about any new problems, I usually ask parents to tell me about what's been going on at home. Mrs. Allen told me that they'd had a family gathering and her son had seemed a little upset and frightened around his grandmother, who'd been sick. She also told me she had been to a teacher conference at the boy's school and that his teacher had been pleased with his progress. It's always useful for me, and gratifying for parents, to talk about all the ways in which a child is getting better.

I filled Mrs. Allen in on her son's last session, telling her that he had seemed very interested recently in thinking about separations and good-byes; his play reflected this, and he seemed to be struggling with the issue. In my view, it's not a breach of confidentiality to reveal a child's area of concern, so that his parents and I can understand this together in terms of current or past events. If a child seems particularly worried about something, I'll talk about it to the parents.

Who Sees the Therapist for Parent Sessions?

Both parents are generally seen together for scheduled meetings with the therapist. I find, however, that parents sometimes prefer to explore more private feelings about their children or other aspects of family life individually. Also, when I see a parent alone, I'm freer to discuss controversial areas of his or her parenting without worrying about my comments becoming future fuel for marital fights, rather than helpful exploration.

In Jack's case, I decided to schedule a private meeting with his father, Mr. Simpson, because I felt that what I needed to discuss with him was quite private; it may have been a source of tension in his marriage, and since I planned to talk about his own disappointments and the overlapping of his difficulties with his son's, I wanted him to be able to hear what I was saying without feeling defensive.

I knew that, like his son, Mr. Simpson had an explosive way of dealing with frustrations in his life, and I felt that for the benefit of Jack, who was working with me on finding a new coping style, this was something his father and he needed to discuss. It was courageous of Mr. Simpson to face the reality that as a very important person in this boy's life, his model was contributing to his son's outbursts. Jack adored his father and was very influenced by him. I felt that Mr. Simpson needed to let his son know that this wasn't how he himself wanted to be and that he was sorry he hadn't worked on this problem when he was Jack's age; that it's easier to reverse these things when you're still young.

In my experience, because children want to be loyal to their parents, they feel guilty about being different from or better than them. Although Mr. Simpson didn't bring about any magical change in Jack through their conversation, he did give him the message that he could be like the kind of person his father valued and admired, rather than exactly the kind of person his father was. Giving a child permission to find a better way of dealing with things frees him to grow into his own person.

Seeing parents alone is also a good opportunity for me to get to know them as separate people, particularly in terms of their own family life as children. For all these reasons, I sometimes schedule parents separately, with more frequent sessions being scheduled with the parent who has primary care of the child.

Other Caretakers. It's important for me to have some contact with all of the main caretakers in a child's life, so that I can learn about him from various perspectives and try to give suggestions wherever possible on how to handle the child. I'll always try to speak with teachers as often as needed, and if a child spends a good deal of his time with a baby-sitter, grandmother, or other caretaker, I might want to schedule one or two sessions with this person.

Sometimes it's enough for me to communicate by phone with a person who is a secondary caretaker. Betty, for instance, spent her days with a baby-sitter who lived too far away to come to my office. I spoke to her at length by phone a few times, and she gave me invaluable insights into Betty as she saw her, removed from her home environment.

Parent Sessions and Divorced Parents

I already told the story, in chapter 2, about the divorced and remarried mother who called to make an appointment for a consultation with me about her child, Sophie. Because I was worried that Sophie's biological father would be made to feel like an afterthought, I told her that I preferred to wait for him to return from his business trip and see me before I would meet with the stepfather. A couple of weeks later the mother called back to cancel the appointment. It turned out that her ex-husband was opposed to the idea of therapy and so her daughter, realizing that this was going to be yet another hot issue between her parents, didn't want any part of it either.

Problems can develop around parent-work involving divorced parents, especially if there's ongoing animosity between them. In my experience, when only one parent works with the therapist, there's a danger of the other parent deciding that the child's therapy has nothing to do with him, that it's not something he wants, or even that therapy is worthless. In cases of joint custody, a parent might even decide to stop his child from continuing treatment.

These kinds of problems, while understandable, are potentially damaging to children. In the best interests of the child, therapy should not be linked to either parent. Children must be allowed to see the therapist's office as neutral ground, as separate from their parents' battles and not associated with the conflicting tugs of loyalty from which children of divorce suffer.

I always advise parents that, for the sake of the child, if they disapprove of therapy, they should quietly discuss their reservations with the therapist or their ex-partner. If a child is in therapy, it's essential that he be allowed at least the illusion of harmony on the subject between his parents.

Some divorced parents have no problem coming to joint parent sessions. For other divorced parents this kind of working together around the child's therapy is counterproductive, if not impossible, because too many bad feelings between them get in the way of useful discussion about the child. If this is the case, just try to let your child know that you are both working with the therapist, and are both involved in his treatment.

Stepparents. Whether or not stepparents are included in the initial sessions depends on the situation. As I mentioned in Sophie's case, I would try not to see a stepparent before a biological parent unless there were unusual circumstances—for instance, if the biological parent lives far away, or if everyone (including the biological parent) acknowledges the stepparent as the one who has assumed all real, practical parenting functions. As one little boy said, "When someone gets up out of bed in the middle of the night to hold a bowl for you to throw up in, that's your father."

HOW CAN THE CHILD THERAPIST HELP PARENTS DEAL WITH TROUBLESOME FEELINGS?

When parents are troubled by specific feelings about their handling of, or reaction to, their own child, these feelings can usually be dealt with in parent sessions.

Understanding Your Initial Feelings About Your Child's Problem

When parents first start coming in to see me after their child has started in treatment, I generally find that there are some initial feelings they have about what's happening that they need to address.

Many parents, when they first come to see me, are troubled by feelings that have developed in response to their children's difficulties. Sometimes these kinds of feelings are a way for parents to protect themselves from the distress that they inevitably face when they see their child constantly in trouble, always sad, or angry and bitter. Examining and clarifying the feelings often softens their impact. A better understanding of your child's emotional difficulties and their causes can provide relief by putting things in perspective.

Single parents especially can be burdened with a whole array of worries, because they often have nobody close with whom to share their concerns. Sometimes a single parent will bring a child in for treatment and, as treatment progresses, it becomes obvious that she is terrified about the future. Robby's mother, for example, who had been left alone to care for her son when her husband died, was obviously scared about how she was going to deal with everything as the years went by. She told me, "I can't even begin to think about adolescence." It was a huge relief for her when she realized she would be able to come and see me, on and off, as long as she needed to, and that just knowing this might relieve some of the anxieties of single parenting.

Some parents come to their first parent meetings in torment over a whole combination of difficult feelings—guilt, anger, shame—some of which they've been carrying around since their children were babies. Mrs. Rosen, the mother of a four-year-old boy, Paul, said to me when she first came to my office, "It worries me—I think I hate my child. We hate each other." Of course, she felt terribly guilty about her feelings.

She explained that Paul was intensely attached to his father, and that every time his father had to go away for his work, Paul would be deeply upset and would give her a very hard time. Mrs. Rosen told me that she just ended up getting angry all day and feeling out of control. When she wouldn't let Paul do what he wanted, he'd tell her, "You're the worst mommy! You don't know how to do it right!" His words hit her right where it hurt, because she didn't realize that this was just a very smart four-year-old doing his version of "I Hate You." She believed him; she agreed with him; she, too, thought she was the worst mommy.

I had to help her be a mother by reassuring her. She was hardly the worst, but she was very insecure and she needed to be reminded that Paul was no authority on parenting, but just a little boy who needed his mommy to be in charge. Sure enough, as Paul's mother took control of the situation and her guilt and anger eased, they were able to develop a strong, loving relationship.

Don't hesitate to discuss any of your worries with the therapist, however shameful or petty they may seem—worries about your child and her future, about money, about what other people will think, what to tell the school, what your child can tell his friends. The therapist will help you address such worries in a realistic manner, so that you can concentrate on the main problem.

Guilt. In my experience, guilt and shame are among the most common, and perhaps the most painful, feelings experienced by parents whose children are entering therapy—"I've failed. Look at my child, it's all my fault." Not everybody feels this, but many do; don't be surprised if you do, too. It's very easy to feel that you've failed in your role as a parent. And when your child is troubled, it's an easy way of explaining to yourself all the things that have been going wrong at home.

The fact is, however, that many factors determine how a child grows up. You can often see it in your own family; children can be quite different from birth. You remember David, who was too fragile to be able to deal comfortably with his life at home—his brother, who was after all growing up in the same environment, with the same parents, just laughed at the same stressors; he was born with a different temperament and had developed different coping styles. There are so many things that are different for different children as they grow up, and parents don't actually have the power to totally create or destroy a human being.

Of course, things that you do as a parent do have an impact on how your child develops, but it's never such a clean, one-to-one connection. I also point out to parents who are feeling guilty that they cared enough to want to help: they're in my office, where our goal is to make things better.

Denial. Perhaps you have been playing down your concerns about your child, not to others but to yourself. Watching a child be in trouble can be so upsetting to parents that they sometimes deny there's a problem: "It's just a phase." "It's not serious." "It'll pass by itself."

This happens especially when a teacher or guidance counselor has referred the child. Perhaps she seems just a little difficult at home, yet the school keeps calling you in to discuss her behavior problems. Then you might convince yourself, "It's the school's problem; my child is fine."

Other times, one parent feels that it's time to talk to a therapist, while the other parent resists and denies, saying, "Oh, no. I was that way myself at this age and I outgrew it—he'll get over it, too." It's a comforting thought, but it doesn't allow anyone to work on the problems your child is facing.

Anger. Anger toward the child is another initial feeling, like denial, that parents can use as a way of avoiding the real problem. Your anger means that you think your child's symptoms are deliberate and within his control; he's just being naughty, and you want the therapist to help him "shape up." By feeling this way, you can imagine that your child's behavior is outside the realm of emotional disturbance.

However, as long as you're not using it to avoid the problem, anger is a perfectly natural reaction—he's disrupting family life, his tantrums make every day a nightmare, he's a troublemaker in school, he's just trying to annoy you. An angry parent is often a helpless parent: Helplessness quickly leads to frustration, which in turn may express itself as anger.

Confusion. Many parents come to their first meetings filled with confusion and anxiety about their child. They don't understand what's happening. All they can think is, "Is my child disturbed?" "I've been such a good parent—how come this child is so unhappy? What's wrong here? Is he going to be like this forever? Can my child ever lead a normal life?" A real answer has to feel better than this.

Parents are also confused about the cause of their children's troubles. Guilt can lead you to oversimplify the connections between cause and effect—"If only I'd waited to go back to work until he was in school all day," or "I should never have yelled at him those times he wet his bed"—leading to yet more guilt.

One of the first ways in which a therapist can help you feel less troubled is by providing clear information, when possible, on the nature of your child's problem: how simple or complex it is, how transient, how common, how treatable, and how it should be handled. Don't always expect precise answers; the course of treatment is an ongoing process, with the child, therapist, and parents learning increasingly more about this complex young person and his difficulties.

You might ask yourself, "I've been such a good parent, I've given him everything he needs; how could this happen?" Aside from dealing with the troubled feelings underlying this question, a therapist can help you see the connections between your child's innate temperament, his particular needs and struggles, and the match between his personality style and your own.

Feelings That Emerge
While the Child Is in Treatment

Having a child in treatment can stir up feelings that weren't present when you entered this process. As treatment progresses, it's not uncommon for a parent to feel competitive toward the therapist or to blame someone in the family for a child's problems.

Parent-work can feel like a very blameful experience. In helping parents to help their children, I have to make parenting suggestions about styles and techniques that might work better for a child—and inevitably parents feel guilty and ashamed. It's important to address these feelings, because if you're blaming someone (maybe yourself) for your child's problem, or you're competing with the therapist for your child's affection, then it's very difficult to feel sure of your ground in your parenting.

Competitive Feelings. Anxieties about the child's attachment to the therapist is just one issue that concerns many parents, sometimes from the outset but usually as treatment progresses. As your child settles into treatment and you see him growing very fond of the therapist, you might think, "What if he ends up liking the therapist more than he likes me?" You might worry because you picture your child talking to the therapist about things that he's never spoken about with you. You may even feel left out of this important piece of your child's life.

Children do develop attachments to their therapists; this is an essential part of treatment. And there are certain things that a child can't discuss with his parents (although sometimes less than you might imagine) for fear of upsetting them or being punished. However, it's important to remember that children tell their parents a great deal more about their day-to-day experiences than they tell the therapist. A child may reveal a few secret thoughts to me during play sessions (I am, after all, trained to read between the lines and encourage such revelations), but you are still the one to whom he runs for comfort, or to share his excitement.

Sometimes a child will play on his parents' anxieties by saying, "I like her better than you. She never gets angry. She lets me do things that you won't let me do at home." You have to realize that the child's attachment to the therapist is of a different nature than the child's attachments to his parents. It's a unique relationship; my role is to create a nonjudgmental atmosphere and to give the child my undivided attention. The relationship and atmosphere I create in my office are important to the process of therapy, even if they're not what the child needs on a daily level. Even his tantrums are useful to me, rather than just something to handle, because they tell me something I need to know about the child.

A child might become very attached to me, but it is ultimately a temporary attachment. Eventually, children say good-bye to me and get on with their lives; your child knows, and of course you know, that saying good-bye to his parents would be a very different story.

Shame. Sometimes, as treatment progresses, parents worry that an older child in particular is telling me too much about his life at home. Perhaps he's describing for me the fights between his parents; maybe he's telling me about how hard his father spanked him last week when he hadn't done anything to deserve it.

It's only natural for parents to worry about their loss of privacy. You should remember, nevertheless, that a therapist hears many stories in the course of her practice and is unlikely to be shocked by anything that your child has to tell her. Besides, she's only interested in your private life insofar as it impacts on your child.

Blame. I was once consulted by the parents of a very angry three-year-old boy, John, whose feelings showed themselves in the form of tantrums and a sleep disturbance. John's parents both had full-time jobs, and the boy had been cared for by a succession of caretakers, some not too successfully. The father felt that John's behavior problems were due to the fact that the mother was too permissive; the mother felt that the father was too tough. Through all the blame they both felt like failures.

When parents disagree on the nature of a child's problem, they may both end up blaming each other for what's gone wrong. Each, in turn, compensates for the other; the strict parent becomes stricter, the lenient parent becomes even more so, and as a result the child grows confused and the marriage can suffer. In parent sessions, I try to help clarify such differences between parents and at the same time help them to find common areas in their attitudes.

I saw John's case as one in which the child could be helped

through parent-work alone, and so I proceeded to show the parents how John was responding angrily to the fact that he felt unanchored by any consistent or familiar caretaker, and confused by conflicting parental messages. Another child may have been able to deal with the situation more calmly, but John's symptoms were exacerbated by his intense personality from birth.

During monthly meetings I worked with John's parents on building their sensitivity to his separation anxiety, and on correcting the caretaking situation (by pointing out that it was more important for John to have a consistent caretaker than a perfect one). I also helped them to develop new parenting skills—essentially, how to handle their upset child by becoming clearer and firmer in their approach to his behavior, but more emotionally indulgent. I tried to help the father adopt a softer approach toward his son while I firmed up the mother's style, so that the two would be more alike in their messages to John and John's care would be more consistent.

Although the feelings of blame or guilt that parents can have at the outset of their child's therapy are often softened in the course of parent-work, the reverse can also be true. As I've said, parent guidance can feel like a very blameful experience, and sometimes learning more about the nature and sources of a child's problems only increases the tendency to blame, especially if there are misunderstandings or confusions.

You might blame yourself or someone else. Sometimes one family member is blamed for the whole problem. For example, everybody decides that it's the father's fault because he took a job that requires more traveling; or the mother is too involved with her career to give her child enough attention. Meanwhile, nobody is focusing on making things better.

Occasionally, all the blame is put on the child, and parents expect the therapist to correct the situation without any effort on their part. They deposit the child once or twice a week as if to say, "Fix this." Blame is not what cures the problems. Everyone has to participate in putting things right.

Achieving a Broader View of the Problem

Feelings of confusion and misplaced blame are often alleviated when parents achieve a broader view of their child's problem. My role is to help parents achieve this view, by sorting out the confused thinking that so often leads to blame, and by correcting the oversimplified explanations that can emerge in one's struggle to make sense of something stressful.

Although a child's early experience in his family is undeniably the most powerful factor in shaping his emotional life, parents have to understand that many factors contribute to the development of a person. Taking into account that mothers and fathers do not relate exactly the same to each of their children, it's still interesting to see how differently siblings respond to the same set of parents, or to the same external events such as divorce or death.

Children are born with individual temperaments and certain innate abilities that they take into the world with them and to which the world responds. As children grow, external events shape their perceptions, and experiences outside of the home affect the way they approach life. Perhaps the child had a bad year in school because of a learning problem; maybe he was in a class with a particularly mean group of kids; maybe he gets teased regularly because he's short.

In their early years, children's views of themselves are primarily affected by how they see themselves reflected in their parents' eyes. As their world expands, the opinions of teachers, coaches, peers, and others have an increasingly important effect. Many factors in a child's development are beyond a parent's control: Parents don't, in fact, have the power to create or destroy a human being. The child is his own person—you're there to help him function in the world in which he finds himself, and the therapist is there to help you.

HOW PARENT-WORK HELPS YOU
TO HELP YOUR CHILD

During child sessions I come to understand individual children better, and I use this knowledge to help them grow. But since therapy only occupies a small portion of a child's life, I also use my insights as a basis for enlightening and advising the parents, so that they can help their child at home.

Sometimes parents have to help their child to behave or feel differently: Sometimes parents have to change in the way they handle a child. This might mean learning new parenting skills to deal with specific behaviors, or it might mean a more radical change in parenting style. The main point of ongoing parent-work is to look at the child's world—most importantly, his life at home—in order to figure out what isn't working, and how to make it better.

When you're exhausted and exasperated after months, if not years, of battling with or worrying about a child, and you've tried everything that everyone said you should try to make things better, it can really help to sit back and calmly examine what's been going on. One of the most important things parent-work can do is to give mothers and fathers the power to understand themselves and their children as individuals, and to understand themselves in their role as parents. For many parents, that's one of the major routes to resolving the struggle.

Never before have parents read so many books and articles on child care, attended so many talks, or been so keen to discuss issues with teachers and pediatricians. As a result, parenting decisions appear to be deliberate and well informed (except when you're aware of losing your temper). In fact, your parenting style may well be more emotionally determined than you think. During parent sessions, I try to help parents understand this, so that they can begin to respond more to the real needs of their children rather than to those irrational voices within them.

Voices from One's Own Childhood

The most subtle of these irrational influences on parenting style lies in repeating the patterns of one's own parents. The details might be different, but if you look at your parenting more closely, the essence is often the same as what you knew as a child. Perhaps your parents demanded that you wore conservative clothing; you insist that your child be free to choose, but actually you discourage him from wearing conventional clothes "in the interests of free choice." Are you not, in fact, equally involved in creating a style that meets your needs and not your child's?

This example touches on another irrational influence on parenting—the movement away from, rather than toward, what you knew as a child. The parent who says, "My parents were so strict that I can never be that way with my children," has decided to be permissive without considering the interests of his or her own children.

The story of Mrs. Rosen, Paul's mother, whom I mentioned earlier in this chapter as having difficulties in her relationship with her son, is a good illustration of how one's own childhood experiences, or the worries associated with them, can enter into one's life as a parent. Mrs. Rosen told me the story of how, as she lay in the hospital having just given birth to Paul, she became very frightened that she, like her own mother as she remembered her, would not be able to adequately mother her child.

After returning home, her anxieties grew, until her mother came to visit, and at one point Mrs. Rosen asked her to change the baby's diaper. The mother didn't know how. Of course, this only confirmed how little Mrs. Rosen must have been given by her mother when she was a baby, and it sent her straight into a depression. So the baby's father took over, becoming Paul's primary parent in the early years, and Mrs. Rosen remained convinced that she couldn't be a good mother. All the problems that developed between her and her son stemmed from those initial anxieties about her own capacities, based on her life's experiences.

In fact, there is no reason to believe that one is doomed to repeat experiences from one's own childhood. People learn how to be parents from many sources; you get it from somewhere else if you have to and want to—from a teacher, a friend, an aunt, or just from who you are as an individual.

Irrational Reactions

Earlier in this chapter I mentioned the mother who felt that she couldn't tolerate her child's expressions of neediness. She felt badly about it, but she couldn't help it. It's always valuable for parents to examine why they are unable to tolerate certain behaviors and moods in their children—why, for instance, you get so angry when your three-year-old baby-talks, or when your five-year-old gets away with breaking the rules. It's easier to make enlightened parenting decisions when you've looked into and accounted for your own sensitivities.

Parent-Child Match

A major aspect of my ongoing parent-work is to help parents understand their parenting style in relation to their child's age and temperament. Sometimes the match between parent and child is difficult; your style of parenting may even suit one child in the family but not another. Perhaps this child is loud and aggressive by nature, whereas you are shy and retiring, and so you easily yield to his public outbursts; or maybe you have trouble expressing yourself physically, but your three-year-old seems to need constant hugs to assure him of your love.

A mother once made an appointment to see me for a consultation about her three-year-old daughter, Jane. I saw the parents, and then I saw Jane, and although she seemed to have a highly charged activity level and a very determined nature that needed firm parental limits, there didn't seem to be any serious problems. The little girl left to join her mother in the waiting room, and a couple of minutes later I heard a torrent of screams. I went out into the waiting room, and there I saw Jane and her mother struggling on the floor as the mother tried to make her put on her hat, gloves, and coat. I watched as they wrestled, and knew this had to feel very shameful for the mother. She was a very gentle, introspective woman, and her very active, somewhat aggressive daughter needed the kind of parenting that didn't come naturally to her. Finally, they left with Jane still not wearing her coat—she had won.

Here was an obvious case of parent-child mismatch. Given a child with an average activity level and less willfullness, this mother would have been fine. But she had a very active, persistent child, and active children often have to discharge that energy in an aggressive way. I had to help this mother understand that neither she nor Jane were at fault. We worked together on how she could avoid this kind of conflict with Jane; I suggested, for instance, that instead of struggling for power with her over the coat, she could have simply assumed power by sitting down, picking up a magazine, and telling Jane that they would leave only when she had put on her coat.

I also devised a long-term program with Jane's mother and father. The central task was built around a phrase they could repeat to their child: "You have to learn to stop yourself, and we'll help you when you're unable." That way Jane's task was clearly defined for her—to develop the power to stop herself. It also made her parents' limits and interventions feel less arbitrary to Jane, because they were connected to this task that she knew she had to work on. As she got older and had to learn new limits or master new tasks, these, too, would be connected to the original theme, "the power to stop yourself"—someday, for example, it might be, "I know you're around friends who are drinking or taking drugs, but you have the power to stop yourself."

Match and Age. As children grow through the various developmental stages, what's required of a parent also changes. What worked well when your child was one doesn't apply in handling a four-year-old. For instance, it's one thing to accept the crying of an infant who has no other way to tell you he's upset, but an older child needs to develop internal controls and frustration tolerance.

Some parents feel naturally more comfortable when their children are in certain stages. During these times parenting can seem relatively easy and satisfying, while at other stages it can seem to be a struggle. For instance, a mother might feel entirely comfortable with her child while he's a cuddly, dependent baby with routine needs, but find him hard to deal with as he grows into an unpredictable, toddling explorer and begins to reject her lap. One mother, who had been happily caring for her infant son, began to feel very troubled on the day that she bought him his first pair of shoes. Another mother only started to enjoy her child when she learned to walk and talk and gained some independence.

Learning to Adapt Parenting
to a Child's Needs

Some parents long to be a certain kind of parent in the hope of shaping a certain kind of child, but from the youngest age, that child has a personality and needs that are independent of the parent's ideals. Perhaps you're committed to the idea of giving your child absolute freedom to develop creatively, never realizing that she might need order and routine in her life if she's to feel safe. Or perhaps you want your child to grow into a tough, adventurous type, but your expectations and hopes only make him feel worthless because he's just not that kind of person.

It's also not uncommon to find mothers and fathers trying very hard to be the kind of parents they have always wanted to be, to meet their own ideals of what parenthood should be. But that doesn't always work for the child. For example, the mother of a very hyperactive boy I was seeing once told me that she couldn't bring herself to be firm with her child because it made her feel so cruel and controlling, whereas she had always cherished the idea of being a permissive and tolerant mother. I told her that was not the kind of parent her child needed, and a few weeks later she called to thank me. She said, "That freed me to understand his needs, and not to think about what made *me* feel good in parenting." Particularly when unusually firm or harsh-seeming limits are needed, many parents need support in applying them comfortably.

And yet it isn't always so easy for parents to let go of their ideals. I was once consulted by a family about a child who was wildly out of control. She had always been temperamentally very difficult: She was born into the world fighting, screamed the first year of her life, and soon had the whole family running circles around her. Her mother would yell at her but never could set clear limits. Her father tried to humor her out of her tantrums and let her do what she wanted because he identified with her so strongly. He, too, had been wild as a boy, and he didn't want to be like his own parents, who had, as he saw it, attempted to break his spirit.

Nobody wanted to cross this explosive child. When she finally hit rock bottom by going into uncontrollable rages because she was upset about going back to school, her father decided it was time to set limits. I suggested to him that he tell his daughter, "Things have been so bad for everyone, including you, and I'm never going to let you experience that pain again. That's why I'm going to help you control yourself—I'm going to give you rules."

I felt a sadness in the father as I said this, as if he were about to put his daughter's spirit in irons. I looked at him and said, "Do you think she was a joyous free soul? She was such an unhappy child. She was out of control, everyone was yelling and screaming, she was upset about it, and she needed to know that she could count on you to order her life."

Parent-Child Battles

Quite a few of the stories in this chapter concern battles between parents and their children, and of course I deal with these battles and their causes in the course of both the child's therapy and parent-work. Sometimes it's simply a matter of helping parent and child rediscover their common ground; sometimes it's a matter of helping a parent find a new pattern in some aspect of his or her relationship with the child. In Andrea's case, it was both.

Andrea had been locking horns with her mother incessantly; their relationship seemed to center around little more than fights. The theme of my work with Andrea's mother at this point was, "How could you let her have some things her way, without its interfering with family life?" I felt that by removing power struggles where possible, both mother and child could have some sense of control over events.

For instance, Andrea's mother wanted her to go sailing with the family, Andrea didn't want to, and whenever they planned a day out in the sailboat, a fight ensued. I said, "Isn't this a choice you can allow Andrea to make? Perhaps she's scared of sailing. Can't you give her the choice of sailing, or staying with the housekeeper while you go out on the water?"

I helped them to unlock horns by pointing out to Andrea's mother that there are decisions a child can be allowed to make. It's a matter of thinking to oneself, "Which decisions are parenting decisions and which aren't?" Obviously, a child can't be allowed to go outside on a freezing day with no coat. This is a parent's decision to make, and one can be firm about it. I often suggest that parents frame these moments protectively by saying, "This is something I have to decide so I can take care of you"— to keep you safe, or to keep you healthy, for instance. But if a child wants to wear a blue instead of a red dress, there's no harm done. Even if she doesn't want to sail, as long it doesn't keep the whole family off the water, the child can have a choice.

Particularly with a parent-child relationship that easily slides into struggles over power, it's important to make these distinctions. By letting children decide whenever possible, you can help them to feel less pinned down, less oppressed at those times when you do have to make the decision for important reasons. In fact, when Andrea no longer felt as if she were capitulating to her mother's wishes, she was quite willing to try sailing. Parents don't always realize that a child who's engaged in a struggle for power is really struggling for his life—if he loses the struggle, he feels as if he has lost some piece of himself.

I frequently invited Andrea's mother into the therapy room. I find that sometimes parents and children who are stuck in a pattern of fighting can rediscover each other in a place that's separate from home, and separate from the pressures and triggers that set off the fights. I wanted them to be able to play together, to enjoy each other and remember how much they had in common, to balance out the power struggles they'd been having.

More About Parent Guidance

Parents of children in therapy have an invaluable resource at their disposal—an expert on child development and behavior who can give practical guidance on day-to-day parenting. Because the therapist knows your child, this guidance is specifically designed to suit his personality and to meet any special needs he may have.

Quite often, my suggestions to parents develop out of themes that have emerged during a child's play. I mentioned in the chapter on play therapy that I used the insight I gained into Mary's play with doll families to guide her parents at the next session (this was the child whose play families never included children).

I had spoken with Mary's father and knew that he was very overwhelmed by what it meant to have children. He had never imagined how it would really be. He said, "I thought if we had kids we could take them along and do everything we'd always done in the past."

When Mary's parents came to see me, I told them that there was something in her play that suggested to me that she felt her life at home did not accommodate her. We talked about their life and how this insight might apply. In some way, perhaps Mary's feeling was true. Most children feel this at times; Mary probably felt it more than some (although her parents were very loving) because of the extreme pressures in her life. Their life was so busy and overbooked that there was no room for normal, childish interferences.

I told them that children often feel very pressured by a life where they can't just sit in front of the television on a Saturday morning, or mess around with crayons, or just stay home and be crabby; where they're always having to quickly get up and get dressed, so that everybody can get out the door and into the car in order to go off to do something. Although the parents were giving their children some wonderful things, they also needed to give them time for the more difficult sides of childhood.

Practical Guidance. Jack seemed to have an intuitive sense of how I, as a therapist, could give his mother clues on how to help him in his difficulties. Although he knew his parents were in regular contact with me, and that I was giving them advice, he also wanted his mother in the room with us while we worked. She would watch me deal with his rages and help him out of them, she saw how I calmly encouraged him to organize himself and his thoughts, and as time went on, she learned to integrate what I did with what she found useful in her own way of parenting.

Practical guidance is an important aspect of parent-work. By incorporating the therapist's recommendations into your parenting, you not only support the treatment your child is receiving during her regular sessions, but you unify the messages for development she receives in different parts of her life.

Generally, I'll guide parents in handling a problem at home on a practical level, while I deal with it during child sessions on a more in-depth level, but the messages are still related. A little girl with a toilet-training problem, for instance, spent child sessions working with me around the theme of being scared to grow up. When I saw her parents, I gave them basic advice on toilet training and sent them home with a doll and potty game to play with their child. In this way, two important segments of her world—therapy and home—were united in encouraging her to feel safe about moving forward.

MAKING THE MOST OF PARENT SESSIONS

You can take full advantage of parent sessions by coming prepared to ask questions and receive information. This may sound obvious, but in fact I find that parents often find themselves at a loss during sessions, searching their memories for all the little things they had meant to ask about. Then, maybe a week or two later, they find that their recollection of the suggestions we discussed is not altogether clear. This can happen very easily when there are long intervals between parent sessions.

You can make better use of parent sessions if, whenever something comes up at home that's not urgent enough to warrant a phone call, you simply make a note of it. You might want to keep a notebook handy to record incidents or jot down questions. Even though you think you'll remember these things, it's very possible that two or three weeks from now, when the time comes for your meeting with the therapist, other issues may have taken your mind off the earlier questions.

This same notebook can come in useful during the session itself, for recording the therapist's recommendations. Very often so much information is given during a parent session that, especially if you're feeling anxious about your child, it can be very difficult to remember everything exactly.

Taking notes of recommendations and explanations can help you remember and can also help you to clarify the information you're receiving. The therapist might use terms or phrases that you don't fully understand; if you don't understand it, you won't be able to put it down in note form. Then is the time to ask for a clearer explanation.

Phone Contact—When to Call

Regardless of the frequency of scheduled parent meetings, as a parent you should have phone access to the therapist. Call for advice on specific problems that can't wait until your next meeting: How do I tell my child that his grandfather died? The baby-sitter to whom she's so close is suddenly leaving—how do I deal with it? What problem signs should I watch out for? However, if it's not urgent, if it's just another tantrum or just another wet bed and you and the therapist have already discussed it, then you should wait until your next scheduled meeting.

You should also use the phone to report anything that the therapist should be aware of when she next sees the child—things that are happening at home or in school, whether you're anxious about some new development in the child's behavior, or you simply want to report an event that you feel the therapist ought to know about or that might be upsetting the child. Perhaps the child's father is going away on a long trip, perhaps there has been a change in child-care arrangements, perhaps the child has suddenly started stealing, or fearing school. This differs from what a child might see as tattling—reporting about how bad she's been without adding any new information.

The therapist can advise you by phone on how to handle a difficult situation, or support you in an action you've already taken. I was once working with a small boy, Ian, on developing his capacity for self-control. The three calls that I received from Ian's mother over a period of several months perfectly illustrate various reasons for phone contact with a therapist. The first call was for an urgent talk to discuss some possible sexual abuse of the child. The second was to get my reaction to a note she had already written to her son's teacher, in which she had wisely requested that Ian be given a new seat in class apart from his disruptive neighbor. The third call was just to leave a message letting me know how things were going at home with a plan we had devised to help Ian develop better controls. She added that this call required no response from me.

One of the purposes of parent-work is to help you develop a sense of your own effectiveness in dealing with your child. Eventually, you may feel less need to consult with the therapist by phone. When something worries you, try to think what the therapist would tell you to do, or what your own intuition suggests. You may find that by now you've absorbed much of the therapist's thinking as a supplement to your own, adapted it so that it suits you and your child, and that you have the confidence to deal with the situation without the therapist's help.

PARENTS' RIGHTS AND RESPONSIBILITIES

Ideally, the parent-therapist relationship is a collaborative one, in which both are involved in learning about your child and bringing about growth. A two-way flow of information is essential. As a parent, you should see this as both a right and a responsibility. It's your job to help the therapist to help your child by keeping her informed about things that are happening at home and in school; by following up on her recommendations, as long as you agree, for special services such as tutoring or speech therapy; by carrying out the parent-guidance suggestions on which you've agreed with her; and by communicating with your child's teacher about school-related areas in your child's course of treatment, and any special recommendations that the therapist has made if the therapist hasn't communicated these directly to the school.

Here are some of the other areas in which I feel parents have some responsibility toward their child's course of treatment.

Appointments

A father whose child was in treatment with me would repeatedly cancel sessions and say, "We just needed a break," or "He was upset," or "Something was happening in church." He was frightened that he was forcing his child into something he didn't want to do. He'd already had to force him into a consultation, and now the boy was resisting treatment. I knew he enjoyed the sessions once he was in the room, but he was the kind of boy who would fight his parents over anything new, so of course he fought over going to treatment.

I finally said to the father, "You have to bring him, even if he puts up a fight. You have to give him the message that this is something important in his life over which he doesn't have a choice. Tell him that there are some things that children can't decide. Otherwise he'll just keep fighting. He might seem to be upset, but he'll adapt."

Therapy is a health decision, and health decisions are not a child's to make. It is your responsibility as a parent to support your child's treatment by making and keeping appointments with the therapist. Therapy sessions should become a regular part of your child's life, not to be neglected in favor of play dates or because the child is tired or reluctant to go.

Respect

It's important that you speak respectfully of the therapist in front of your child, both as a professional and as a person. Don't let him hear you talk about how silly her dress looks, or how her office needs repainting, or how you're not sure whether she's doing the right thing. The therapist is becoming an important person to your child. Don't confuse him with your comments, even if they're only meant jokingly.

School

Some children who are in therapy have no school-related problems; school is a place where they do very well. But many children's difficulties are played out in the classroom and schoolyard, in which case parents should talk this over with the therapist.

It is your right to expect that the therapist will make every effort to collaborate directly with the school if any school-related problems arise during treatment. Usually phone contact with the school is enough, though I occasionally arrange to observe a child in class so that I can better work with the teacher in developing strategies to help him overcome his difficulties. The source of these difficulties may be self-evident, as in a child with poor internal controls or attention problems. Or they may be more hidden; for instance, children often express their separation anxieties through anger or oppositional behavior in school, in which case the therapist's insights can be very helpful to the teacher.

Schools generally welcome suggestions from the therapist, and often become calmer and more willing to work on a child's problems when they are being supported by the family and a professional. Parents who feel uncomfortable about the school being brought into the therapy process should discuss this with the therapist—but remember that the benefits are far greater than any embarrassment you may feel.

Confidentiality and the Parent's Right to Information

Naturally, parents have a great desire to know what's going on in an important area of their child's life. You have a right to the therapist's view of your child and the course of treatment. She should discuss with you the goals of treatment so that you can come to an agreement on what you're working toward, and have some sense of what constitutes finishing. She should also fill you in on how treatment is progressing, and you can expect her to explain why, for instance, nothing seems to have been happening in therapy for some time, or why your child appears to be going through a period of regression.

It can be hard for parents to accept, however, that they do not have a right to know what specifically goes on during a child's therapy sessions. In my experience, some degree of confidentiality for the child is essential if I'm to establish a safe, trusting environment in which children feel free to say or reveal anything—including information about their parents or life at home—without worrying about the repercussions. Even some very young children value this privacy.

Although you don't have the right to specific information from the therapist about what your child does during sessions, she might offer to tell you about something that happened during a session if it makes a point without revealing anything confidential—this depends on the style and judgment of the inividual therapist. But even if the therapist does tell you, "He seems to be upset about school," you should avoid relating this to your child or questioning him about it.

Of course, the degree of confidentiality varies according to the individual therapist, and also according to the child. Some children love confidentiality; they won't say a thing unless they know it's a secret. Even at home, a child might more readily pull one parent aside and tell him some bad things he's done, making him promise to keep it a secret, than talk about it to both parents; it works the same in therapy. Other kids don't seem that concerned, and many are just as happy to reveal themselves when their parents are in the room. With these children I might ask their permission to divulge some specific revelations when I think it will be useful in parent-work—"Can I show this picture to Mommy and Daddy when they come?" "Can I tell Mommy the story you made up?"

Even when children don't immediately seem to care about the things they say getting back to their parents, I try to ease them into a more private kind of session because I know that in the long run they might need that sense of privacy. For the same reason, I usually suggest to parents that they don't probe too much into their child's experiences in therapy. This doesn't mean that you can't in any way discuss therapy with your child. You can ask him general questions, such as how he feels about being in treatment, but you shouldn't ask him about what went on during a session, and neither should you encourage him to offer information.

Therapy works best when a child sees it as his own, private domain. If, near the beginning of treatment when there's little of a confidential nature happening, your child seems to want to share his therapy experiences with you, you might suggest to him that, while you're very interested in what he has to say, there may well come a point when he prefers to keep his therapy private, and therefore it might be in his interest to start out that way.

What children do during therapy is also protected by the rule of confidentiality. If a child were to curse or write on my wall during an angry outburst, that would be between him and me, to be used in the most helpful way possible; he shouldn't have to worry that I might report his behavior to his parents.

If you can respect the confidential nature of the child-therapist relationship from the start, as difficult as this often is, you'll find that it pays off in the long run. While you may feel excluded from the therapy room, you have a large share in your child's growth as a person.

5

❧

PROGRESS, REGRESS, AND GOOD-BYES

S ome children respond quickly and consistently to therapy, with improvements at home and in school showing up within a relatively short time, and parents feeling increasingly pleased with the results of treatment. Quite often, though, change isn't so fast to come, nor so clear-cut. You might have to wait very patiently for any signs that your child is feeling better. The tantrums might go on for a long time, teachers could continue to complain about behavior or attention problems in the classroom, and it might begin to seem as if life with your child will never be free of worry. Things may even take a turn for the worse from time to time, with any gains lost, and more. None of these factors mean that therapy isn't working.

Nevertheless, it's only reasonable for you to wonder, "How can I tell whether my child's treatment is going to help eventually, or if it's never going to help at all?" You might ask yourself if this is really the right therapist for your child. You might contemplate giving up on the whole idea, especially if you're having to drag your reluctant child to the therapist's office week after week, as occasionally happens.

All sorts of worries and discontent about your child's progress in therapy can arise. There might come a point where you feel that therapy should be finished, because things seem to have worked out so well and your child is surely better, yet in the therapist's opinion your child needs to stay in treatment for a while longer. Or maybe the therapist tells you that your child is ready to end treatment but you don't think he is, and the thought of what life is going to be like when he's no longer in therapy only makes you more anxious.

It's very difficult for a parent to begin sorting out these worries without some understanding of the course that treatment usually takes, and it's important to appreciate not only the course of treatment—in other words, the typical rhythms of the therapeutic process—but also the importance of letting treatment run its course. It's easier to be calm about what's happening as your child moves through therapy if you understand that regression is often a part of moving forward. And it's reassuring to know that, although at times treatment can seem to be moving very slowly, this doesn't mean that nothing is happening.

THE PHASES OF TREATMENT

A child's treatment tends to move in phases. Of course, there can be variations, but most of the time there's what I call an "introductory" phase in therapy, during which a child settles in and forms a relationship with me; an "exploratory" phase, during which we look a little beneath the surface of day-to-day issues and try to find new ways of feeling and functioning in the world; a "consolidating" phase, when the child starts to fix those changes as part of her new self; and a "termination" phase, during which the child is weaned from the therapeutic relationship.

Phase One: Getting Comfortable

Parents tend to think that nothing is really happening during the first phase of therapy, but in fact there's a great deal to be learned from how the child starts treatment. It's particularly important for a therapist to learn about how a child deals with the beginnings of relationships or situations, since in real life the beginning affects everything that follows.

As I've said in previous chapters, the way the child enters therapy or doesn't enter, the way he resists or is suspiciously eager, the way he protects himself from his anxiety at being in a strange place with a strange person, or shields himself against any kind of personal revelation—all these things tell me something about who the child is and how he lives his life. The child who cries and holds back every time she has to enter my office, for instance, or the one who begins therapy as if it were a honeymoon—by being the "goodest" child in the world while she's in my office and keeping all her tantrums for home—is giving me valuable information about herself.

Nonetheless, although I'm learning a lot during the first phase of treatment, most of the work that I can do with some children during this period is very much on the surface. Angry David, for instance, had a long honeymoon period; he spent an entire year being very good, although I was getting reports of severe tantrums and constant difficulties at home. We got a lot done during this year in the sense of supportive therapy, talking about David's strengths, discussing how kids can get along with each other, and helping him to feel good about himself. But I knew that I wouldn't be able to help David very much until he stopped being so good—until he knew that he could bring into my office the rages and tantrums and bitterness that he was showing his parents at home, so that I could understand him better and figure out how to help him.

David was coming up to first grade, and his school was wondering whether they'd be able to keep him in a first-grade class that had less room for his kind of nonparticipation than the nursery program. Although they reported that he seemed to be calmer on the days following his sessions with me, he still spent most of his time standing in the back of the classroom, refusing to participate. In other words, in over a year of therapy there seemed to have been very little in the way of visible progress. That's when I bought the Oscar the Grouch doll for David so that, speaking through the doll, he might be able to share with me the bad-boy side of himself without having to worry about my not liking him. Only then, as we entered the eye of the storm, would we be able to look under the surface and start exploring feelings.

Many children feel compelled to protect themselves against their anxieties about therapy, whether by closing up as David did, or by kicking and screaming. Although it may take a long time before these children look as if they've settled into treatment, don't be fooled into thinking that this is just a preliminary period. For some children, the most critical part of our work is being done at this time. Their very resistance, whatever form it takes, is what interferes with them moving along developmentally in *many* areas of life; they cope with their anxieties through defensive behaviors. The point when they can allow themselves to lower their defenses and cooperate is a milestone in their progress.

This doesn't mean that you, as a parent, should try to push your child into cooperating; she's just doing what she feels she has to do. A large part of the therapist's work during the first phase is to create an environment and a relationship which allows the child to learn new ways of coping with her anxieties.

At the same time, David's case should not suggest that all children get stuck for so long in the introductory phase of treatment. Some children, like Mark, the little boy who insisted the walls were black, for instance, make the transition into the second phase of treatment far more readily. Mark was careful with me for a while, during which time I did a lot of work helping him be more tolerant of himself—"People can't be perfect," "Everybody makes mistakes, but they can still be terrific"—so that he could see that I would tolerate his flaws, and in turn so that I could soften his harsh judgments of himself. As soon as he felt comfortable with me and understood clearly that this was a place where people with problems are accepted, he started to bring in the power games that he was playing with his family at home. With this, we saw the end of Mark's introduction to therapy.

Children who resist coming to therapy pose a real problem for their parents. They might say that they hate therapy, or that they don't like the therapist, and of course after a few weeks or months of this, parents start to wonder if they made the right choice. Usually, though, there's some other reason for a child's resistance, which the therapist will be able to explain. One nine-year-old girl, for instance, kept insisting that she didn't want to come to her sessions with me. I knew it had something to do with the fact that because therapy had not been her idea, she felt that she had no control over this part of her life. Since we obviously weren't going to get anywhere as long as she felt this way, I gave her the option of cutting down her visits to once, instead of twice, a week; sure enough, her attitude toward treatment changed and she managed to move forward quite fast. Other children, like David for instance, never stop saying that they hate coming to therapy, yet once they're here they obviously enjoy it.

Michael, on the other hand, was very frightened of being close to anyone besides his parents and wouldn't let me get close to him. It wasn't until the moment that I asked whether he might feel more comfortable if he could be the boss of how close I got that his turning point came. Although his anxiety about people was a long-term treatment issue, this brought down his anxiety to a level where he could tolerate staying in the room with me, instead of having to leave early.

Occasionally a child will begin to feel and act better almost immediately upon beginning treatment. Robby, for instance, whose mother had been left to parent him alone when his father died, thought that he had to be the man of the house now. As he started treatment, he seemed to feel a huge sense of relief merely from the fact that there was suddenly another adult sharing the burden of parenting—almost like a new and supportive family member. As soon as there was this extra support, he felt able to release those feelings of grief that he had kept bottled up since his father's death. Children of divorce can show the same kind of response to the beginning of treatment.

Phase Two: Exploring the Inner World

The second phase of treatment focuses on the child's developing self-awareness. I've already talked, in the chapter on play therapy, about the kind of work that I do with children as we explore their inner worlds of feelings, beliefs, and self-image. And you'll have seen in that chapter how we work on finding new ways of coping with troublesome situations, so that avoidance, rages, or aggression are slowly replaced by behaviors that don't backfire on the child, and that feel more comfortable.

Nearly all children who are initially resistant to therapy manage to relax and open up after a while, allowing some kind of deeper work to be done. The frightened child no longer needs to have her mother or father in the therapy room with her (not all therapists allow this, but I feel that in some instances it helps things along until the child is comfortable with me); the resistant child begins to yield to the relationship, as did provocative Betty, while the "best" child in the world starts to react to the therapist in the same way that he reacts to members of his immediate family, and becomes his normal, problematic self.

Buying the Grouch doll for David sparked off this exploratory phase. David started to bring into treatment all the stuff that he was showing his parents at home and sometimes his teacher in school. At first his mother saw this as regression; he had been so good in my office, and now he was being so bad. But soon, as he brought his tantrums to me, he began to seem quieter at home, and he managed first grade in school.

Why did it have to take so long to reach this stage? A child can't be hurried into the second phase of treatment. Exploring feelings takes a certain amount of strength. Sometimes I have to wait until I feel a child is strong enough to look inside, and to make connections, before I can start helping her to understand herself. In one case, it took two and a half years before the child reached this point—Michael, the boy who felt so uncomfortable alone in a room with a non-parent that I had to relate to him from the safe and fixed distance of my gray chair for a year and a half before he could finally feel safe enough to let me move around the room. Before this, treatment was all directed toward strengthening him, keeping scary thoughts at bay and feelings in check. Only when he was stronger and older could we start doing some exploring.

I remember the day I first made any reference to the way Michael was feeling, having decided that he was ready to start looking at himself. He was sitting on the floor by the toy closet, tossing toys forcefully around the room, and I said to him, "I'm wondering if that's something you do when you're feeling angry?"

Michael didn't say anything, but I suddenly realized that there had been a shift in this very active child's rhythm. I looked at him, and he was slumped on the floor; he looked completely crumpled, as if he'd had all the wind knocked out of him by this comment, which felt like such deep criticism. I said, "Michael, do you think I could like a boy who throws things when he's angry?"

"Could you?" he asked me very tentatively.

I said, "You bet your life I could!"

He lit up. "You bet your life! Your life is such an important thing! If you bet your life, then it must be true!" After that, Michael started to get used to my observing him and noticing things about him, and as he felt less threatened by it, I was able to talk to him more and more about the way he felt and the way he dealt with the world.

Children reach this point in different ways, but most reach it at some point, and it's a milestone in their treatment. When a person finally takes the lid off what she's been thinking and feeling, and is heard with calm understanding, there's a huge sense of relief, which continues as we start on the gradual road to self-awareness. Not surprisingly, this can be a period of blossoming, although there may be regressions, too, as I'll describe later.

Usually children do the reporting about his day-to-day life during the introductory phase as a way of growing comfortable enough to explore deeper fears and feelings about themselves. But one nine-year-old girl I was treating, Melanie, got there after a long time in a fascinating kind of reverse sequence, and proceeded to show me a part of herself more buried than that which most children bring to treatment.

Melanie was such a closed and terrified child, with such a damaged self-esteem, that if another girl came up to her in the classroom and made an overture of friendship, she became so anxious (because she couldn't trust that the person really liked her) that she'd have to move away. For a long time in treatment she was so exquisitely sensitive to the possibility of anything being personally revealing that she couldn't even tell me the simplest, day-to-day things of her life. She wouldn't tell me that she was having trouble making friends. She did a lot of drawing, she made up games and designed clothes for her dolls, we made up a play and invited her mother in to see it, but she would never sit down and talk about anything remotely personal. Once, when she had to miss a session, she told her mother to tell me that she had a cold, rather than tell me the real reason that someone close to her had died and that she had gone to the funeral. That felt too emotional and private.

One day, Melanie was looking at some notebooks in my closet and asked me what they were for. I told her that these were books in which I wrote notes when I saw my adult patients, and I asked her, "Would you like to be one of my adult patients?"

Melanie agreed, left the play table, and lay down on my couch. I asked her what her name was and she sneezed, so she decided that she was going to be Mrs. Choo. She started talking, conveying to me a life of one of the most disgusting persons who ever lived. She talked about husbands who had abandoned her, about how she was so unlovable, so fat and ugly. All her worries about herself were suddenly given free rein. Once again, through the third person, a child was able to handle the pain she felt by projecting the most shameful parts of herself onto "Mrs. Choo." Then they belonged out there, to someone else. As a therapist, I understand that her most inner, private, irrational worries about herself were being expressed through the disgusting, distasteful adult she had created. I had never entered a stranger world with a child.

Melanie went away on summer vacation after the Mrs. Choo session and I wondered how she should deal with coming back to treatment. As she walked in for her first session after the break, I didn't say anything, wanting her to set the tone. She said, "Well? Aren't you going to ask me how my summer went?" And from then on she talked—about friends, about rejections, worries, her parents, all the things that I needed to know, that she had been unable to tell me for so long. Perhaps she felt that I would be as accepting of her as I had been of Mrs. Choo.

In all three cases—David, Michael, and Melanie—the children were able to reveal unacceptable aspects of themselves and to have the therapist accept and sometimes clarify those aspects. In turn, the children could more easily live with themselves and could possibly also modify certain aspects of the way they acted.

Phase Three: Growing Into the New Self

When David came back from his summer break to resume treatment for the third year, he had his final tantrum in my office as he dealt with the fact that, despite all his resistance to growing attached, he was so happy to be back. He never had a tantrum in my office after that. For David, this was the beginning of what's known as the consolidating phase. Things had stabilized after the changes that had taken place within him.

During this phase of his treatment, David's calm had a whole different meaning than it had in the first year. It no longer meant "I'd better not show her how bad I am or she won't like me," it meant that he felt at peace during treatment, with himself and with me, and that he felt stronger because he could truly handle what was inside of him. He remained calmer at home and at school, too. I had shown him what made him feel bad, what made him feel better; now I was no longer trying to move him along so much as watch the growth settle in and become permanently his. Now David could tolerate losing at games; he could tolerate losing games with me, and could even let me win points in games he had created once in a while. Although his growth in this area lagged somewhat outside the treatment room, he was no longer so desperately holding on to the things that made him feel good about himself.

It's important to remember that although children can seem better fairly quickly in the course of treatment, and can have seemed better for several weeks, this doesn't mean that their new behaviors or their new ways of coping with the things that cause them stress are truly theirs yet. That's one of the reasons I tell parents that they shouldn't pull a child out of treatment at the first signs of improvement, however jubilant they feel about the changes. Until a child has really internalized her new ways of looking at herself and dealing with life, so that they feel more part of her than the old ones, she can all too easily slip back.

During the consolidating phase of treatment, I also have a chance to work with children on fine-tuning their gains. If you remember, Stephanie needed some help in learning how to relate in an unbossy yet deliberate way with the new friends she was making. One seven-year-old girl, during the last phase of her treatment, said, "I understand—it's like when you make a table, and the table's really made, but then you still have to sand it and smooth it and take off the rough edges." Until a few months earlier, this child had always insisted that she preferred to play alone, and had isolated herself on the school playground every day. Now, toward the end of treatment, fine-tuning consisted of helping her figure out how to recognize that another kid was interested in playing with her, and how to join a group of kids at play. Once a child has reached the point of refinement, it's only a matter of time before I plan the termination of treatment.

Phase Four: Saying Good-Bye, and After

The termination period is a very important phase of therapy, even though by this point parents and their children can sometimes feel "enough is enough." Besides the fact that there might be some unfinished treatment, therapists have ways of "weaning" a child from therapy during this final phase—an obvious example is to introduce a period with fewer visits.

Many of the children I treat have a particularly hard time with separation. Just as I can learn a lot about a child by seeing how she begins her relationship with me and therapy, the end of that relationship offers me a way of showing her that she is able to say good-bye. Good endings to treatment also help children leave therapy knowing that their relationship with the therapist is still intact, and that she is still there if they should need her.

A good illustration of the importance of respecting termination as part of treatment is provided by Ian. His mother called me about two months before he was due to terminate treatment, to say that since Ian hadn't been wanting to come for some time, and seemed to feel quite strongly about it, she had decided not to bring him back for any more sessions. She said she was very happy about how much progress her son had made and didn't see what a few more sessions could add.

We talked a little about why Ian didn't want to come anymore—how much was it that he really preferred to stay home and catch up on some of his favorite TV shows or that, knowing he'd be finishing soon, he preferred to be in control of when? Neither of us felt that Ian had developed any kind of aversion to therapy.

I told his mother, "He's really done very well here. This is something to celebrate! If we just end it here, it's as if he's sneaking out the back door. He should be walking out of the front door with a diploma in his hand!"

I suggested she tell Ian that many boys feel this way about not wanting to come to treatment anymore, and that it was perfectly fine for him not to come since we had planned to stop soon anyway, but that he should come and say good-bye because everything had been very successful. I said, "Even if he can't do it because he's a child, at least he'll know that everything's okay, that the door's still open and I'm not angry at him for wanting to stop." The next day I got a message to say that Ian would be coming next week. He came and said good-bye, and I pointed out to him how many nice things had happened since we had known each other, and how much good work we had done. He seemed very grateful for that, and left in good spirits.

I feel that it's very important to respect the relationships in a child's life. Sometimes parents think that they can spare their children pain by snatching something important away from them, making the process of letting go quick and clean rather than dragged out. It happens with toys and dolls, and it happens with people, too—I once treated a child who had been too quickly separated from the nanny who had cared for him since birth. Children have to be weaned from their attachments. They need a prolonged period in which they can prepare mentally for separation, and they need the rituals that usually go with good-byes.

Separation is one of the major emotional tasks challenging people throughout their lives, and is the source of a lot of appropriate, and sometimes unnecessary, pain. Separating from the therapist is almost like a laboratory situation for learning, with someone's help who knows and understands you, how to handle separation. Children learn that it's normal to feel sad about saying good-bye, but that the feeling gradually wanes. I often suggest to parents that they tell their children when termination time comes, "I know that saying good-bye is sad, but soon you won't feel so sad. You may feel sad when you think of the person, but you won't feel sad every day anymore." The termination phase in therapy can be a learning experience that the child can carry with him through all the good-byes to come.

The Weaning Process. With young children, who don't really have a solid sense of the passage of time, I usually wait until there's a manageable number of sessions left before announcing termination. At some point earlier than this, when I have some sense that the end of treatment is within sight, I'll often ask a child, "Did you ever think about how long you're going to come here?" I want to let them know that there is going to be an ending. Usually they say, "No" or "Forever." They just assume that therapy, and our relationship, is going to last forever. Four-year-old Mark said anxiously, "Do we have one more visit?" He thought I was about to announce the end of it all. I said, "We have lots more time left. You're going to be finishing your nursery class, and you're going to be going to day camp, and then sometime in the middle of the summer we'll be finishing." Betty answered my question by saying, "Always," and then caught herself yielding to the attachment and added, "but I don't ever want to come again."

When there are about six sessions left, which is nearly all a young child can hold in his head, we make a calendar together and I draw six suns, which the child can cross out one by one, after each visit. The calendar gives children a sense of control over something they're upset about, and concretely organizes time for them.

Sam got very excited by his calendar when I first introduced it to him. He went running out into the waiting room to show his mother and explained the whole process to her. It was only when he came back the next week that he realized he couldn't add more suns. Another little boy, Paul, wanted to do his own drawing; he drew the first few pictures, but when he got to the fourth picture, he drew a person with an arrow through his heart. I said, "I guess that's what it feels like to have to say good-bye." He couldn't finish the pictures until he came back the following week. Two years later, when Paul came back for a visit, he told me that he still had that calendar hanging on the wall above his bed.

REGRESSION—TWO STEPS FORWARD, ONE STEP BACK

Some children simply blossom and grow through the course of treatment, but usually things don't work out so smoothly. Parents are confused when their child, who's been doing so beautifully in treatment for months, suddenly starts throwing tantrums again, or wetting the bed, or even develops brand-new symptoms. Mark, for instance, went through a stage when, to his parents, it seemed as if he were worse than ever.

Children *can* regress during treatment. Sometimes it's because they would have regressed anyway—something's going on in their lives that has nothing to do with treatment. As I described in chapter 1, all sorts of circumstances can lead a child to revert to her old ways, regress in the course of her development. I once received a call from the mother of one little boy who had been in treatment with me and was doing very much better both at home and in school. She sounded very confused; her son was home with the flu and had suddenly gone right back to where he had been before treatment started. What was happening? Was it all lost?

I reassured her that her son's regression was only temporary. Children often regress when they're sick, as at any time when they're home with Mommy for a while instead of going out and functioning in the world. Another little boy, for instance, who had finally started to use the toilet went back to his diaper during the summer vacation months. Sure enough, both children reestablished their gains when they went back to school.

Regression as Progress

At other times regression is a part of progress itself. Mark's regressive behavior, for instance, occurred around the time that he was trying out some new behaviors with me—allowing me to win and to be right, allowing me to help him, and allowing himself to experience me as the stronger one.

The same is true in many children's treatment; it's like a storm before the calm. Why did Mark, and other children like him, have to revert to his old ways of dealing with things at home just at the point when therapy seemed to be showing some progress? I believe that it was because he was being asked to give up his old ways of coping, of feeling better about himself: When you ask any person to give up their unsuccessful coping habits, they're left for a time with no familiar way of dealing with the things that trouble them, only new behaviors that feel like part of someone else.

It's a little like the principle we find in child development itself. If you remember, in chapter 1 I talked about the developmental seesaw, in which children are periodically thrown off balance as they grow into new and higher stages. In treatment, when children experience this gap between the things they have given up and the things they have not yet learned and established as parts of themselves, they might feel anxious and overwhelmed. Mark felt in limbo. He could allow himself to feel safe in my office because it was a carefully created environment devoted to helping him feel that way, but at home life was fraught with real-life stresses and demands. Although during these transitional times parents might start to despair of their children ever getting better, I find that this is precisely the point at which I can often move in and help them develop.

Sometimes you see regression in a child who's doing well in treatment—so well, in fact, that he's suddenly freer to let certain things emerge that he had previously kept under a tight lid. I told the story in an earlier chapter about a little girl, Rebecca, who started therapy with anxieties around separating from her mother but, as these anxieties eased, started to act very defiantly; this girl suddenly felt free to let her parents know how angry she was with them about certain things, because she was no longer worried that they were going to abandon her. This kind of positive regression is usually fairly brief.

Other children starting treatment are described as clingy, uninterested in making friends, and possibly school-phobic. They're very fearful of the outside world; nevertheless, these children are very agreeable at home and pose very few problems. They might not fight with their parents, because they are so dependent on them. Then, at some point during treatment, all of that changes as the child starts to differentiate himself from his parents and develops more of a sense of himself as an individual. He might start to act like an oppositional two-year-old who's just realizing he's a separate human being or, like Rebecca, he might finally feel free to express long-harbored grievances. From a parent's point of view, this can seem like regression—"He was such an easy child even if he was a bit clingy, and now he's so difficult. He wants everything his own way; he won't cooperate anymore." In fact, like many forms of regression, this is really a sign of progress.

Regression During the Termination Phase

The termination phase itself, with its painful good-byes, can bring on temporary regression in a child. After I had announced termination to Betty, for instance, she went through a couple of difficult sessions where she was more angry at me than she had been in recent months, and more clingy at the same time. This kind of regressive behavior might cause you, as a parent, to wonder if this is really a good time to stop treatment. One mother called me in a panic shortly before her child's last session to tell me that he had been behaving with a lack of control that was reminiscent of his earlier levels. But as we talked about it, it became clear that, along with the child's anxiety about terminating treatment, he had been overtaxed that weekend. The boy had been functioning quite well for six months, and just as I expected and, in fact, reassured his mother, he didn't get stuck in his regressed state. At times like this you shouldn't feel that your child's regression means that she's back at square one, and it also helps to reassure the child of the same thing—"Even grown-ups sometimes have hard days."

Once in a while a child, particularly a child with self-doubts, takes termination as a rejection. When this happens, there can be severe regression. When I told Mark about finishing treatment, for instance, he looked a little unhappy but he didn't say anything, and during the next two sessions he looked fine, although he seemed a little quieter.

The third session came, and suddenly Mark announced to me that he was now "Mr. Nice Man." He was being very polite, in almost an exaggerated way. That day I was talking to his mother, who was worried about a severe sleep problem Mark had been having very recently, and I mentioned the Mr. Nice Man incident. She immediately said, "I'll bet he thinks that if he's nice enough, then he won't have to leave therapy." I thought his mother was right on target.

The following session Mr. Nice Man was literally carried into my office by his sitter and put to bed on my sofa, where he slept deeply through the entire session. He had managed so little sleep for so long. When Mark came for his next session, he was still not sleeping well at night and he was still being extremely polite. So I started to ask him directly about his feelings around leaving. He seemed more amenable now to discussing why he thought he was stopping, and how he felt about it. I looked at him and said, "Mark, do you think that if you're nice enough, then you won't have to leave?"

He looked me right in the eye, grinned sheepishly, and nodded his head yes.

"Mark," I said, "when you go, I'm going to miss you very much. One of the reasons you're stopping is that you've grown so much you just don't need my help anymore!" He looked up at me, and his grin spread from ear to ear, lighting up his face. The next morning I spoke to Mark's mother and she said, "He had his first good night's sleep, and when he got up in the morning, we all celebrated!"

Even after a child has left treatment, she might have the occasional "relapse." The mark of treatment, in my opinion, is not that children will never regress to old behaviors and feelings, but that if they do, they're much more resilient in the face of it because they have new strengths to draw upon.

EVALUATING YOUR CHILD'S PROGRESS

Given all the slow periods and the regressions that are often part of the therapy process, how can you know whether or not treatment is likely to yield results? The best option, in my opinion, is to discuss any anxieties you might have about your child's lack of progress with his therapist. If she is unable to reassure you, or she herself says that things aren't moving along as well as they should be, then it's time to consider a second opinion (I'll talk about that later).

As a parent, you can't always expect to immediately see clear signs of the progress your child is making in treatment. Children usually start to change in my office before they bring those changes home with them. The therapy room is almost like a laboratory setting where children can try out new behaviors and get used to them before testing them on the world at large. Therefore, if I see change happening in child sessions, I can share this encouragement with the parents.

It's very hard to know what exactly causes change. Sometimes there's sudden progress because of things that are changing in a child's daily life, or because of a natural growth spurt. In fact, it can be hard to separate out a child's natural growth—the growth spurts that are part of normal development—and the growth that occurs as a result of the child's treatment. They function as partners. When a child is unstuck, his natural developmental thrust fuels his movement in therapy. At the same time, therapy itself enables a child to have a developmental growth spurt; if he hadn't been in treatment, growth in a particular area might have been blocked.

One of the marks of progress in therapy that doesn't depend so much on the child's natural thrust for development is in the parent-therapist relationship. You should feel that therapy is helping you to understand your child's problems and your relationship with him. If you don't feel that this is happening, or if you have serious doubts about the therapist and her approach to treating your child, then you should talk it over with her.

Is It Time for a Second Opinion?

If you have the feeling that nothing has happened in therapy and a great deal of time has passed—certainly a year or so—discuss it with the therapist. If she can't help clear up your anxieties, you're free to seek out a second opinion.

Many factors might contribute to your dissatisfaction. One time, for example, I was consulted by some parents whose child had been in therapy for a year and a half, and who weren't at all happy with how things had been going. It turned out that they really didn't like this therapist, nor did their child like treatment with him.

I spoke with the therapist at length to hear his view of how things were going, and he agreed with a few of the parents' concerns. Balancing out the various facts—that the child had shown little growth and that neither parents nor child seemed comfortable with the therapist after one and a half years—I advised them to move on in the interests of a better match.

Before you decide that you don't like a therapist or the way she's treating your child, you should try to consider the reasons for your feelings. Is it that you really don't like this therapist because of the way she's treating your child, or because something she's telling you about you or your child is making you anxious, or because you just don't like the idea of your child being in therapy? Or is it that, whether the treatment has been effective or not, there simply is not a good therapist-parent or therapist-child match here? A consultation with a second therapist can help you sort out the answers.

When the Child Decides She Doesn't Like the Therapist. Sometimes parents feel like quitting because suddenly the child says she doesn't like the therapist, and even seems angry at her. But sometimes this dislike is just a factor of the child settling in and beginning to transfer to the therapist some of the negative feelings that she has about close relationships outside of the therapy room—an important phase of therapy because it lets me look into those feelings. At this point you need to talk with the therapist to see if this might be what's happening. I also point out to parents that a child who fights his parents over everything will also fight them over the issue of therapy; in other words, you can't take an oppositional child's dislike of his therapist as the final word.

Finding a Second Opinion. Of course, seeking a second opinion means looking for a therapist whose opinion you can trust, someone with a great deal of experience to draw upon. I should point out that in seeking a second opinion it's wise to consider the personal bias of the person with whom you're consulting. You should try to find somebody whose approach to treatment is roughly compatible with the approach of the child's therapist; for instance, if he has been seeing a play therapist, don't consult with an expert in behavior modification or psychoanalysis. In addition, you should always tell your child's therapist before seeking a second opinion.

Is It Time to Finish?

One of the most helpful ways of gauging when your child might be ready to finish treatment is not through calendar time, but by considering your goals. As you've worked with the therapist and she's worked with your child, you've probably refined your idea of what the goals of the treatment are, and what kind of change is reasonable to expect. At some point it will feel as if your child has reached that goal. Once in a while, on the other hand, parents and therapist can't agree on the time of termination simply because they're not in agreement on the goals. If you feel that this is the case, it would be wise to talk it over with your child's therapist.

The main objective of treatment, in my opinion, is for a child to be stabilized and on the right track so that parents can continue the work at home. One little girl, for instance, had done very good work during her nine months of treatment, but one critical, final issue remained to be tackled—she was still very aggressive and oppositional in the classroom. I told her parents that I felt she should come back after the summer for a couple of months so that I could help get her on track in this area while she settled in with her new teacher; beyond that, I saw it as a parent-teacher job. In other words, she didn't have to resolve this problem completely in order to finish treatment, but the major issues in her life had to have been addressed to the extent that with the help of her parents she could keep moving in the right direction.

If You Decide to Quit

Sometimes parents have a very realistic sense of their child's progress. A mother whose child had been in therapy for four years once called me for a second opinion. She felt that her son had made all the progress he could be expected to make; his behavior seemed to have stabilized, and she was happy with the outcome. Between the time of the phone call and our appointment, this mother made up her own mind to discontinue treatment. I told her on the phone that it was very important to give her child some way of adequately saying good-bye to therapy and the therapist—after all, four years is a long time in the life of a child.

This is just as true if you have decided to switch therapists, rather than leave therapy altogether. Whoever that person is, and however much the child may have disliked treatment with her, it's important to teach a child that relationships are something to respect and value. The message should be that people are not interchangeable: "Perhaps this didn't work out the way we were hoping it would, but this is still a person who's been nice to you and has cared about you, and you can't just walk out of it without a good-bye."

SAYING GOOD-BYE
Coming to Terms With
the End of Your Child's Treatment

Quite often a strong attachment forms as parents and therapist work together to help a child, and although the focus of termination obviously centers on the child's responses to separation from treatment, you as a parent also should be prepared to miss the therapist. Part of it is that parents get scared of the idea of losing the support that a therapist provides for their parenting. But a larger part of it is that, like their children, parents grow attached.

I mentioned earlier that part of the point of parent-work is to help parents come to a point where they have the confidence to handle difficult times with their children, rather than depending on the therapist. David's mother was very nervous about his finishing treatment. She said, "You mean we have to manage alone with our child?" I told her that I would still be available to her, that she could call me or come in anytime she needed, and that David could come back and visit if the need arose.

I felt that after three years of treatment David had grown a great deal. He fully participated in school, with just an occasional "hard day" when he would become withdrawn. He got along with the other children, and tantrums ceased at home and elsewhere. Things had stabilized in his life and no new areas of work were coming up in treatment, so I didn't feel that a fourth year was justified.

Nevertheless, a few days later I received a worried call about David from his father, who told me that David had had two tantrums in the last few days because his team had lost in baseball. How, his parents wanted to know, were they going to deal with no therapy?

I reassured David's father that this was a father-son issue. "You're his baseball person," I told him. "Here's what you have to do: Put your arm around David and take him for a walk. Don't criticize him for the weekend—just tell him that you're really pleased with him because he's learned his batting, he's learned his catching, and now he's ready to learn something new called sportsmanship. Tell him, father to son, that you're going to pass this on to him and work with him on this, and that you know he can do it." I told David's father that this was clearly something to be handled between father and son.

Post-Therapy Follow-Up

You'll probably have gathered by now that the termination of treatment is not necessarily the termination of the case. Many of the children I treat leave therapy with some fragilities that I expect might cause them some difficulties once in a while; parents, too, often need further help as their children develop and face life's challenges. That's why I often feel it's important to make the option of follow-up work a formal part of the treatment plan; at the very least it's understood that "I can continue to be an ongoing resource for you and your child."

Sometimes I feel a child is ready to quit therapy but still needs a more proscribed form of support for a specific problem. In the case of Michael, for instance, who was learning disabled, my feeling was that so many of his worries had been laid to rest and that his anxieties at this point were nearly all connected with how bad he felt about his schoolwork. (I knew that with each new grade in school he would come up against this problem.) It seemed to me that at this point Michael would get as much help from an expert in the field of learning as he would from coming to me, so I recommended that he start remediation—a very comprehensive and sophisticated form of academic help, beyond tutoring.

Once in a while, if for one reason or another they're feeling especially stressed, children themselves make the connection between seeing me and feeling better, and they ask for a visit. Over a year after Andrea finished treatment, for instance, something very tragic happened in her life. Right after this happened Andrea started talking to her mother about visiting me. Her mother called me and we set up an appointment—we called it a "visit" so that Andrea would differentiate it from a treatment session. Since the appointment was two weeks away, I asked her mother to leave a message on my machine, just before the visit, letting me know how Andrea was doing. I had decided that if she was dealing with the event by herself, then I would not bring it up unless she did.

Sure enough, the message came that Andrea was doing very well. She came to my office and played, going through all the toys she knew and liked, seeing that everything was still the same, and then she left. Clearly she had laid her own crisis to rest, but she needed to feel reassured and to know that things were as she had left them should she have to return.

Termination doesn't mean that things are neatly finished. My own feeling is that people stay who they are, but who they are doesn't have to interfere with their lives so much. Betty, for instance, will always be somewhat provocative, but she'll no longer have to deny her attachments to other people. During her last session, as we were drawing good-bye cards together, I heard a very quiet little voice say, "I like you." Just like that, very matter-of-fact. I knew how hard it must have been for this child to say that.

Stephanie was doing very well at home and with her friends by the time she finished treatment, yet the way she dealt with termination reminded me of the flavor of our earlier interactions. When I told Stephanie that she would soon be terminating, she said, "We can't stop." I asked her why and she told me, essentially, that our relationship was too important. Then all of a sudden, a few weeks before her last session, Stephanie came in and told me that she loved her new tutor and didn't care much for me. Although she had grown considerably, she was in this case still her old avoidant self, preferring to invest herself emotionally in a relationship that was not ending, rather than deal with one that was. She did, however, allow herself to experience some attachment in our final session.

David, who had made the deliberate decision never to tell me things about his life, and never to show me he cared about anything, continued to do so until the very end. And yet, however many times he gave me his standard message of "I hope I never see you again," by the end of treatment the look in his eyes, his voice, his wanting extra time each session made it clear how sad he was about saying good-bye.

A couple of weeks before our final session, I asked David if he would like to take the Grouch home with him to keep, because this doll had been such an important part of his treatment. I told him why I was offering it to him, and exactly how the Grouch had been used to help him tell me about himself. I made sure that everything we had done and everything he had accomplished was brought firmly back to him. I reminded him how we had talked about grouches, and why they have to pretend to be grouchy, and how they think others feel about them. He listened closely, and I could see that he understood perfectly. Then he said, "Well, maybe my little sister would like it." Of course, he couldn't admit to wanting to keep the Grouch for himself, and by this point he was a real expert in the use of the third person!

At his final session David went straight to the closet where the Grouch lived, pulled him out—and clearly it was no longer his sister who wanted this doll, it was David himself. This time, instead of insisting that it was good to be finished with treatment, he looked up at me and said, "The Grouch still cheats, you know."

6

❦

PARENTS SPEAK

Having a child in therapy is by nature a private and solitary experience. Parents don't generally compare notes on their children's treatment or their own meetings with the therapist the way they would talk about, say, their toddlers' finicky eating habits. Yet it can be enormously useful and reassuring for a parent considering or involved in child therapy to hear something from others about the experience: Why did they decide to seek treatment for their child? How did the child respond to the idea and to treatment? What problems did they come up against, and how did they resolve them?

As a way of providing you with a view of child therapy from the other side of the desk, I decided to interview a small selection of parents who have gone through the process. Many of the issues that parents run up against are touched on in these four interviews. One mother, Sheila, speaks about the dilemma of trust: Do you trust the professional, or your own intuitions, when it comes to evaluating the progress your child is making in therapy? Joanne, whose son entered treatment as a result of a divorce, discusses the issue of confidentiality for the child, and talks about financial pressures leading to termination of treatment. Helen addresses the question of when a parent should consider switching therapists, and describes her experience of clinic practice as compared to private practice. Lucy talks about how she felt when her daughter's school strongly recommended treatment for her child, and about the consultation process.

I should point out that these parents are describing treatment with professionals other than myself, so they're able to speak quite freely. I'd also like to make the point that in each case, the experience was shaped by many personal factors beyond the realm of these interviews. Everyone coming to therapy brings their own private meanings, and their own motivations and constraints, both practical and emotional. Nevertheless, although no two experiences can ever be the same, I hope that the more universal issues illustrated in these stories will help to normalize and bring to life a subject that has been for too long shrouded in mystery.

• • •

Sheila's daughter, Lisa, entered therapy at the age of nine. After more than two years in treatment, Sheila began to have serious doubts about its effectiveness—doubts that eventually led her to terminate her daughter's treatment with her therapist, and to look for another professional whose approach would be more suited to both herself and Lisa. I asked Sheila to begin at the beginning, with the circumstances that led her to believe her child needed help.

SHEILA: At the age of five, when I filled in my daughter's school application, I wrote at the bottom: "Lisa is the happiest human being I know." Whether this was true at the time or not, I did at least perceive it as such. But when Lisa was nine, I realized that this certainly was not true anymore. I think she wanted me to know how unhappy she was. There was a lot of sullenness, squabbling, resistance, foot-dragging, defiance—even when she was clearly bored with being defiant. There were increasing comments from her that nobody at school liked her; the phone wasn't ringing a lot and she was obviously having tensions with other kids. Here was somebody who had obvious intellectual gifts and many other kinds of gifts—basic pizzazz and energy—that were being subverted.

NORMA: When did you finally decide to consult with someone about Lisa?

SHEILA: It took a while. It's so hard to surrender your child to other authorities. For a long time I thought there were real-world fixes that could make everything okay; I didn't see the problem as being Lisa's internal relationship with herself. Her father had left when she was about eleven minutes old. I had remarried someone with whom she originally had what I thought was a wonderful relationship—a relationship that deteriorated—and I felt that if I worked on my husband and got Lisa more used to having a little brother, which obviously she was having a hard time with, and if I saw her through all this with extra love and attention, it would be okay. It took my brother and sister-in-law saying, "Dammit, this kid needs therapy," to make the move in the first place.

I asked several child psychologist friends of mine for recommendations, and when three out of five of them said that Dr. Cray was the absolute best, I saw him. He himself couldn't take Lisa, but he did say that this was an unhappy child who deserved therapy, and I took his first recommendation, a highly respected woman with training in the field of child treatment.

NORMA: How did you present therapy to Lisa, and how did she respond to the idea at first?

SHEILA: There was no resistance at all. I didn't present it as, "Do you want ice cream for dessert?" I said, "Honey, this is something that some smart people think we ought to try." She liked Dr. Cray, and then she liked the therapist, Dana. But now, in hindsight, I realize that I didn't like this therapist the very first time I saw her. At the time, I thought it didn't matter that I didn't like her. All these people I respected had said that she was the best, and she had impressive credentials. But now I think it matters a lot. I know that in the course of therapy you may come to loathe and detest your therapist, but the first take should not be one of unease.

NORMA: Did the therapist give you much sense of what was happening in Lisa's treatment?

SHEILA: No. We talked on the phone occasionally and we met sporadically, sometimes with my husband. She also met my ex-husband. But in hindsight I was never comfortable with her attitude. It was like, "Leave the driving to me." Occasionally she would murmur a suggestion at me—"Lisa needs more limits"— but she didn't expand on it, nor did I ask her to because I didn't really assume that it was her function to give parent guidance. But when I did have questions, it was hard to pin her down. She was very elusive, and the attitude she projected was, "You can't really know what's going on here. I, the expert, have to be in charge of things, and if I told you more, you wouldn't understand anyway." And I guess I swallowed that a little; after all, I live with someone whose work I can scarcely understand.

I think the most useful thing Dana said to me in the course of my daughter's treatment was, "You and Lisa would both benefit if you had therapy." So I found myself a therapist, and ironically it was he who helped me to disentangle from Dana.

NORMA: When, and how, did you come to the decision that this was the wrong therapist for you and Lisa?

SHEILA: About six months after I started treatment with my own therapist. Somehow, his being so nondoctrinaire made me realize that I did not have to accept Dana's rather constricted view of how things had to be. And Lisa did not seem to be showing the benefits of someone who was seeing a therapist twice a week. I knew not to expect a quick fix-up job. Although of course every parent hopes that therapy will make their child easier to live with, I understand that the main thing was for Lisa to get to the point where it was easier for her to live with herself. But the real-world results that were supposed to reflect internal change were not happening. Lisa was not so seriously disturbed that after two and a half years there shouldn't have been some glimmer of change.

NORMA: Did Lisa still seem happy to go to therapy?

SHEILA: She didn't resist, she just seemed to accept it stoically. On the other hand, I didn't expect her to come home and say, "Gosh, what a fun session I had today!" Therapy is hard work. I knew that for it to be successful she was going to have to see things in herself, and things about me, that were going to be exceedingly discomforting for her, and that she would have to get beyond that. That's part of what the whole process is about.

NORMA: When you realized that things weren't working out in your relationship with Lisa's therapist, and possibly in Lisa's relationship with her, too, what did you do?

SHEILA: Well, since I could never get anywhere in a conversation with Dana, I went back to Dr. Cray. I told him, "I don't think that what's supposed to be happening is happening." And he said, "Oh, of course it is." The gist of it was, "What do you know about this? This takes a long time, I sent you to someone who's fantastic, and therefore it's got to be okay." I can see that I have trouble with self-described authority figures; this did not do anything to make me happy. And at the same time my therapy was making me realize that the process did not have to be arcane and mysterious, and so overly subtle that nobody seemed to be getting anything out of it.

My therapist talked to Dana several times and told me that she certainly seemed to have Lisa's best interests at heart. But he confirmed that I had the right to feel uneasy, and the right to question if I thought it wasn't working, and the right to suggest that her way might not be the only way or the best way for my daughter. Not every therapist, however brilliantly qualified, is the right therapist for any one person.

So I called Dana and went to see her. I told her that I had great respect for her work, but that I didn't feel as if anything was really happening. She was very defensive at first, but finally she conceded that maybe things were moving along a little slowly. It was hard for her. Then she tried to throw the blame at me by saying that it was my fault for not having given her Lisa three days a week.

So I raced home and called my therapist—"Is she right?" If she'd had Lisa three days a week, would everything have been different?" He told me that there are people who insist on this, but they're not the only people who are right in the world, and that I had been right to insist that part of what my child needed was a life in the real world as well as life in the therapist's office.

I went to Dana again and told her as gracefully as I could that we were going to have to end the relationship. She said she was sorry and that she felt that in time she might have helped Lisa, who was being terribly resistant, to see what she had to see. She asked for a month, and I said, "Of course." She also recommended other therapists who she thought might be suitable.

NORMA: How did Lisa feel about leaving this relationship?

SHEILA: Very happy! Once I was unhappy and began asking her questions about how she felt, she told me, "I don't know if I'm getting anywhere." So she, too, was being kept in the dark about the process. Maybe neither of us heard everything that the therapist had to say; I'm willing to admit that there are complexities. But having switched to somebody who communicates with everybody, I realize what a mistake it was, knowing my particular givens, to put my particular child in treatment with someone who kept so much of the process to herself.

I think that my daughter, like me, needed to be more enlightened about what was going on. And she needed that basic trust that would allow her to talk to the therapist about something that was on her mind. One of the key things Lisa told me around this time was, "You know, there are lots of things that I can't tell Dana." There wasn't trust there.

NORMA: Had you already found her new therapist?

SHEILA: No. I decided I was going to see about a million and a half people this time. Therapy is a major commitment in time and money, so I took my time. I ended up with someone who was recommended by someone who was recommended by someone who was recommended—I think it was the fourth generation of recommendations. I talked to about twenty people on the phone. This time I trusted myself to find someone I felt comfortable with. By asking just a few questions, I could tell a lot about each therapist's flexibility, their warmth in general. I learned a lot about them through their descriptions of themselves and how they work. I knew that I must not have someone who was theory-bound. I was waiting for the click—it's like falling in love. I knew what I had to feel, and I knew that I would know when I had found it. I remember sitting in somebody's office and having the absolutely heartless feeling that "I'm going to say no to this woman. And that's all right."

I was also looking for someone who was right for Lisa. I know my daughter pretty well, and I looked for someone in whose office I thought she would feel maximum ease and freedom. So when I found the right person, I told Lisa that I felt she was the one, but I let her make her own judgment, too.

NORMA Besides the insights you gained into the child-therapist and parent-therapist match, was there anything else particularly valuable in your experience that you think might be helpful for other parents?

SHEILA: I think that it can be a terrific help for a parent whose child is in therapy to have his or her own therapist. For one thing, it keeps you from needing to use your child's therapist as your own. And I think it's helpful to have at least been in a therapeutic relationship, so that you know what to expect. I'm very grateful to Dana for that. I think that she felt I would be a better mother to Lisa if I worked out certain things of my own. I think it's helpful for Lisa, too. It's nice for her that she's not the only one in the family.

What's important to note about Sheila's experience is that although she did everything properly—she consulted with a highly respected person in the field and got the name of a professional with superb credentials—it didn't all work out fine. Fine credentials in psychotherapy are not the pointers to success that they tend to be in more medically based branches of treatment. In these other branches, the issue of relationship—the compatability of personalities—can be seen as a luxury. For example, you might say of your dentist or surgeon, "He's so competent, I don't mind that he's hard to talk to," but in a therapy situation, the personal relationship is key.

As Sheila discovered, credentials are important, but they're not enough, because in psychotherapy relationship is not a luxury, it's a tool. Sheila didn't trust her own reactions to the therapist. She had to find out through experience that not only does there have to be a good relationship between therapist and child, but the parent also must feel comfortable enough to do the essential parent-work. It's even possible that children pick up subtle cues about their parents' feelings regarding the therapist (even from their lack of discussion about their feelings).

• • •

About a year after her divorce, Joanne's four-and-a-half-year-old son began a course of play therapy. Noah was in private treatment for one year.

NORMA: Joanne, I understand that you sought help for your son around the issue of your divorce. Did you go preventatively, or were there symptoms that were worrying you?

JOANNE: Definitely there were symptoms. Noah's father and I were separated, and it was taking a toll on him. It manifested itself in the following way: He'd feel that he had to go to the bathroom constantly. He didn't feel this at night, and not when we were out of the house, but whenever we were home, and it happened in nursery school, too. He would sit down, get up and go to the bathroom, sit down, get up and go to the bathroom. This would happen ten times within thirty minutes. He never had accidents or wet his bed, he just had this constant feeling that he had to urinate.

We went to the pediatrician and he couldn't find anything wrong. Then we went to a pediatric urologist, who put Noah through a very painful course of tests. It was very hard to see him having to go through this. But there was nothing wrong, and the pediatric urologist recommended a rather well known behavior modification specialist who dealt with urinary problems, especially in boys.

I disagreed with him. I felt that Noah didn't have a behavior problem. I felt it was purely related to stress, and I wanted to get to the heart of the problem.

NORMA: How did you go about finding a child therapist?

JOANNE: I was referred by my own therapist. I had no idea what to expect.

NORMA: What kind of impression did you have when you first met her?

JOANNE: I thought she was very nurturing and caring. I liked the way her office was set up; it was fairly bare, and she had a closet full of toys, construction paper, art supplies, and that type of thing.

NORMA: How did you tell Noah about the therapist before he first met her?

JOANNE: I said to him, "You know, Daddy and I are concerned about how you need to go to the bathroom all the time, and your teachers at school are concerned, too." I told him, "At your age, you shouldn't have to be going to the bathroom all the time, and sometimes things like this happen because of other things going on." I was very careful not to use the words "problem" or "something's wrong." I didn't want to make him feel guilty or responsible, because however much you tell children they're not responsible for their parents' divorce, they never believe it. Then I said, "Sometimes, when there's a situation like this, it helps to go see somebody outside your family. Mommy does it, and Daddy does it," I said, because we were both in our own therapy, "and we'd like you to give it a try"

Of course he didn't want to go, but once he started he never complained. I took him the first few times and then it got so that his baby-sitter could take him.

NORMA: How did the treatment go?

JOANNE: Noah saw her for almost a year, one session a week. The urinary problems dissipated within a very short time, about three months, but it was clear that he had other issues that he had to work on. I think he felt very anxious; he felt my anxiety and his father's anxiety. One of the few things he felt he could control was his bladder.

Noah spent a good deal of time playing with swords, which you can interpret any way you want. The same game seemed to occur over and over. The therapist was the bad guy; Noah was trapped in the corner and it was his job to get himself out. They also played with blocks a lot, and they played catch.

NORMA: What was your relationship with Noah's therapist?

JOANNE: I talked to her every two weeks and saw her every few weeks. She saw me separately from my husband; I really didn't want us to see her together at that point.

The one aspect of it that I didn't like was that the therapist told me, "What goes on between Noah and myself is private." And I said, "What do you mean it's private? That's ridiculous. I'm paying all this money for this and it's private?" The therapist said, "Well, you'll see the results." What I really didn't like was when she would ask me to come in for a session to sit down and talk with her, but she wouldn't talk about anything that was going on in the room with Noah. I felt that she was very good with him, but not very good with me or with his father.

She thought it was just a matter of time before it got worked out. It was a very tough time for me. I think I wanted a quick panacea, but it took time.

The other thing that I was very upset about was when at one point I felt he was ready to leave and she said no. Even Noah said it was time. He never complained about going until the time came that he felt he didn't need to go anymore. The therapist made a very large issue out of terminating. She said he needed six more sessions, and I disagreed. Terminating wasn't a big issue for Noah. This was also a time when I was financially strapped, and I felt that she didn't have enough understanding of this.

NORMA: How did Noah feel after he finished treatment?

JOANNE: He was fine. I think he was happy to be finished. Everything's been fine since then.

I think one of the reasons that Noah has turned out so well is that his father and I never put him in the middle, or let him see us arguing, or fighting about the settlement or anything like that. And we get along fine now. I think that really is the key to his adjustment.

NORMA: How do you think therapy helped Noah, besides curing his urinary problem?

JOANNE: I think what the therapy really did for him is that it helped him verbalize his feelings. He learned to say, "I'm angry," "I don't like it when you do that." At first it was shocking to hear this from a five-year-old, but then I realized, this is what I want!

That was the biggest result. He was given the freedom and the encouragement to say how he felt and not be afraid of it. Not that we ever inhibited it, but somehow he was given a language to do it. He does it with his friends, too—"I don't like it when you say that"—and he's fearless about going up to a strange kid in the playground and introducing himself; I think it really gave him a sense of self-esteem. That was the long-lasting benefit, and I think it remains the hallmark of his personality now.

Joanne didn't feel understood by her child's therapist; she felt left out of a very significant part of her child's life. She was asked to blindly leave her child in a professional's hands, which went against this mother's personal style. Especially at a time when Joanne's own relationship with her child was in a state of flux due to an impending divorce, it must have been very difficult for her to turn her child over to a third person—and yet as Joanne could see, this was a very important time for Noah to have someone outside of the mother-father struggles to talk to.

Joanne really needed a therapist who could create a sense of collaboration with the parent. (It *is* possible to preserve a child's right to privacy without shutting out the parent, as you'll see in the next interview.) On the other hand, there are many other parents who feel more comfortable leaving things entirely in the hands of a skilled and authoritative professional.

Money problems can, at times, be a realistic reason to end treatment. (On the other hand, it's not realistic to end treatment on the basis of a reluctant child's prompting. Children can't judge when they're ready to quit, and often can't foresee the

consequences.) When financial constraints exist, termination
can be a real dilemma for parents; Joanne wisely compromised
with the therapist on the number of visits remaining so that
Noah still had a chance to say good-bye.

• • •

Helen's son was five and a half when he began private treatment
with a therapist. At the age of eight and a half, he left the
therapist and moved into treatment at a clinic.

NORMA: Helen, why did you decide to discontinue your
child's treatment with his therapist?

HELEN: The reasons were very complicated. I was seriously ill and went into the hospital for an operation. When I came
back from the hospital, my son, who before that had said that he
wanted to stay with his therapist forever, said he didn't want to
go anymore.

I hadn't felt comfortable with this therapist all along, so I
had asked my son a few times if he would consider switching to a
new therapist, and he had said "absolutely not." Although I felt
completely in the dark with this therapist, I hadn't wanted to
interfere or interrupt something that might be important.
Obviously there was a bond there.

NORMA: In what way did you feel in the dark?

HELEN: Because he wouldn't include me. We would meet
occasionally, once every few months. He answered my questions
very briefly. My son was in special education and the teachers
were begging to have a conference with the therapist because
they wanted to cooperate and have everybody working together,
but he didn't want to cooperate with the school. He said that he
had had bad experiences with teachers thinking he was trying to
tell them what to do and being resentful. So he thought it best
not to talk to the teachers.

NORMA: In terms of working with you, did he discuss the issue of confidentiality?

HELEN: Yes, he said that the child had to know that what he said in therapy would not be passed on. I felt that he mistrusted me. At one time, my son wanted to know if he—the therapist—was Jewish, as we are, and the therapist wouldn't tell him, which I found reasonable. But when we spoke about this issue on the phone and I said, "By the way, I was wondering, too," he wouldn't tell me either, because I might tell my son— although I had agreed with all his reasons about why he hadn't told him.

NORMA: Why do you feel your son decided after all that that he didn't want to continue with this therapist, just at the point that you were seriously ill in hospital?

HELEN: I discussed it with several therapists, and there are various possibilities. I'm sure there were some psychological reasons to do with my having been sick. It could have been a matter of loyalty to me; I'm sure he sensed from me that I didn't like this therapist. It could also be that he was coming across something that was too frightening to deal with, and he wanted to switch. My son didn't tell the therapist that I was sick, so he got no special support in that area.

NORMA: What did you do when your son decided he wanted to leave his therapist?

HELEN: I told the therapist that I wanted to stop. I said that I thought when the patient decided he wanted to stop, that was a good time to do it. He told me it wasn't so simple, because my son could have just been responding to shock. So we phased it out with a kind of trial period. We told him he would go for one more month, and if by the end of it he didn't want to go, then he didn't have to. But my son counted the days, and when the last day came, he said, "No more."

NORMA: I understand that your son continued treatment in a clinic setting. Some people feel that clinic treatment has a disadvantage in that a parent can't choose the therapist who will treat their child. Did you find that to be a problem?

HELEN: Yes, I did. But within the lack of choice, I did choose. When I met the person they had assigned to my son I said, "No way." I knew it wouldn't work for reasons of personality. I didn't care for her myself, and I know my son.

They insisted that we try, though, so I went for an interview with the therapist and my son, and after fifteen minutes he was out of there—even two years later he asked me how I could ever have thought that it would work with that therapist. So I went to see the head of the program and told him what I thought my son needed, and he found another therapist, a psychiatric social worker who I thought was quite good. They've been quite flexible. I don't feel as if it's a factory; I feel that within the limitations they've been very personal, making exceptions for individual needs.

NORMA: Did your experience of clinic practice differ much from private practice?

HELEN: The structure of the treatment was very similar. But there were differences. For instance, the visit in the clinic has to be exactly forty-five minutes. Also the clinic has many more services available. When my children needed testing, they did it. If we needed to do medication evaluation, they could do it. Where they feel that they're not well enough equipped to handle any particular area, they refer me elsewhere.

NORMA: How would you compare your son's first and second therapists?

HELEN: The main difference between the two is that now we have more cooperation. The new therapist went to visit the school, and whoever needs to be involved is involved. I have regular meetings with her, and a very different relationship from what I had with the first therapist. I don't hear about what my son tells the therapist in confidence, but I get a much better idea.

But I've also learned a thing or two—I've talked to a lot of parents and professionals, I've read a lot, I've participated in all kinds of workshops—so I know what to demand. Sometimes I put my penny in; I can argue about what *I* think.

NORMA: Now that you've found someone you're comfortable with, how important do you think your feelings are, as a parent, about your child's therapist?

HELEN: It's very important, if for no other reason than the child senses how you feel. If you don't like the therapist, it can create a conflict for your child. Children sense it—even if you try to hide it.

Helen found herself in an extremely difficult dilemma, though not an unusual one. Her child seemed very attached, but she as a parent was not comfortable with the therapist. That's why it's so important to handle the consultation correctly—to use it to find out about how much contact you'll have with the therapist, whether the therapist will work with the school, how flexible she is in the way she answers your questions, and so on. If, in fact, you have some mixed feelings about this person, you can always ask to come back for a second parent visit before introducing your child. The therapist's response to your request, in itself, will tell you something about her flexibility.

Perhaps the most important thing that Helen did prior to settling her child in with a second therapist was to find out all she could about the process—through books, workshops, and conversations with professionals. Armed with information, she was able to get for herself and her child exactly what she felt they needed at the clinic—despite the fact that it's harder to do this in a clinic than in private practice.

Without betraying the child's confidentiality, the second therapist managed to include the mother and to allay her anxieties about parenting her child. The fact that this was a clinic, as opposed to private practice, was far less important than the match with the therapist.

• • •

Lucy Garner's experiences with child therapy have centered around two of her four children. Peter entered a year of treatment when he was six, despite Lucy's husband's initial resistance to the idea. When Lucy's older daughter's school recommended treatment, she once again went shopping for therapy.

NORMA: Before we talk about your experience with the consultation process, can you tell me something about what led you to child therapy?

LUCY: I first sought therapy for Peter, who was six at the time. He was a child who I felt needed an outside voice, because his makeup was a little different from the rest of the family's, so he was the odd one out. If I'd lived in a medieval village, it would have been the village priest, or it might have been someone from the extended family, but in this world it's normal to speak with a therapist.

Initially, my husband was resistant to the idea of therapy. Although he's a very reflective man, I think it's almost a male thing to think that airing your problems to someone outside of the family can't help. But he understood that I was in need of having something for Peter, and when I put it to him that we needed a handle on Peter so that we could understand him better, he went along with it, because Peter was baffling to him as well.

For my daughter, Caroline, it was difficult. Caroline was ten, and she had separation issues that reared their head. She had gone away to a sleepaway camp, where she was miserable, but I hadn't realized *how* miserable she was. After I ultimately brought her to somebody, this person felt that it really was very much the camp experience—not that the separation wasn't a theme for her that she would always have to play out.

NORMA: How were the separation issues showing themselves?

LUCY: Caroline wanted me to bring her up to the fifth floor, to the fifth-grade classroom, which was very bizarre. By that point none of the other children wanted that anymore. So I knew it was a little wacko, but that was just Caroline right then. However, the school thought that maybe therapy could help to relieve some of the Caroline's anxieties.

NORMA: So you were of two minds about Caroline's need for treatment.

LUCY: I must say that it wasn't the most pleasant of experiences for me to put Caroline in treatment. I've never been opposed to any of my children speaking to a professional—I'd take them to four therapists a day if I thought that was helpful. But I really felt that the school was blowing it out of proportion with Caroline. I felt that by focusing on it, they were making things worse for a child who was by nature intense and anxious. I felt that her separation problem really just needed to be played out.

The other thing that annoyed me was that I understood that if there were deep seeds to Caroline's separation issues, it was that as a very young girl she'd had twins born on her, and that really knocked her out of the water. Then another baby was born right before she went to camp, and I think she was reliving the whole thing with the twins—something she'd had no control over. I didn't need someone to tell me that. I could talk to Caroline about that, and ask her things, and together it could get thumped out.

In retrospect, one thing I will say is that I was upset as a parent because there is a notion among therapists that if you have two children in therapy, then the family needs therapy. I took that as a failure of parenting on some level. I really felt terrible that if the school saw Caroline as needing therapy, and Peter had been in therapy recently, then maybe there were issues—which of course there are, but I had a great need to feel that our family wasn't any more infested with problems that we weren't solving, thereby hurting our children, than any other family. So going with Caroline to find a therapist became a painful experience.

Nevertheless, I turned to my son's therapist for a referral. I asked her if there was someone close to Caroline's school, because I felt that if Caroline could walk there by herself, it could become her project, and this could help her with a sense of independence.

NORMA: How did you feel about this therapist when you met her?

LUCY: My husband and I went to see her for a consultation, and from the beginning I felt that, although she couldn't have been more sincere, this was not the right person.

NORMA: Where did you go from there?

LUCY: I got another recommendation, someone whom both Caroline and I liked very much. But even so, Caroline remained very self-conscious about being there and wasn't happy about being in treatment. If there was any therapy that went on, it was around getting Caroline to deal directly with the therapist about not wanting to be there.

So after about five visits, we ended it. We had satisfied the school's need to know that we had seen someone. The therapist had by now assured herself that Caroline was not a child in trouble, although she had issues to work on. She also seemed convinced that the separation problem was really connected to the camp experience, because during her visits Caroline described some things that had happened there that I'd never really focused on because they'd never been said to me so clearly. She really had had a terribly rotten time at camp, and just needed to be allowed to act like a four-year-old for a while, which she did and has now stopped.

After Caroline finished, I continued to see the therapist, to speak about Caroine, because we thought that between the two of us we could resolve some of these things. I also thought that this was a time in my life when therapy could help; a lot of my angst over my children and because of my children is my own idiosyncratic makeup, so it was actually a perfect follow-up.

• • •

Caroline's therapy was very short term and the benefits were not the classic "cure." What was gained was that Lucy managed to get a perspective for herself and for the school as to the level of difficulty of her child's problems, and some affirmation that they could be handled at home. In other words, this was almost like a prolonged consultation. Also, Caroline was given the experience of doing something that she was scared to do—she gathered up the assertive powers she needed to get herself out of therapy. Another benefit came from the fact that Lucy chose to continue in her own therapy.

Lucy trusted her instincts during her first consultation about Caroline and wisely chose to go where she and the therapist were more compatible—she understood how important it is for a parent to feel comfortable with the child's therapist. Lucy's family functioned in an active and spontaneous style, whereas the first therapist's style was more formal and reserved. Had this been Lucy's first experience with child therapy, she might not have really known what she wanted or what she could hope to expect. But she had learned through a good prior experience what felt right for her and her daughter, just as Helen had learned through a bad prior experience.

Not every parent with a child entering therapy has the benefit of hindsight. It's for those who might one day say, "If I'd only known," that I hope this book, and these parents' insights, will prove most useful.

APPENDIX A: SHOPPING FOR THERAPY

How does a parent go about finding the right kind of treatment for a child? First of all, there's the problem of how to get a referral that you can trust. Second, there's the question of what kind of setting to seek treatment in, and with what kind of professional—psychiatrist, psychologist, social worker, or psychiatric nurse. There are many factors involved: what's available in your area; how much you can afford to pay; in what kind of setting do you feel most comfortable. Every option has both its advantages and its disadvantages. I hope that this brief look at the possibilities will help you to decide which is right for you.

REFERRALS

I would say that you should first talk to other people whose opinions you value. These could be friends who have had some experience with child therapy, or professionals who know about children. The most obvious examples are the school guidance counselor, your child's pediatrician, or your family doctor.

If you are unable to find a referral through these channels, you can call your county chapter of the American Psychiatric Association, the American Psychological Association, or the Society of Clinical Social Workers, and ask to be referred to somebody experienced in child treatment.

A few organizations can give referrals for children with special needs. These include the Association for Children with Learning Disabilities and for handicapped children, the Easter Seal Society.

WHAT DO THE VARIOUS
PROFESSIONAL QUALIFICATIONS MEAN?

As you start shopping for therapy, you'll quickly discover that "child therapist" is a very broad term. Therapists may be trained in one of a number of different specialized fields or disciplines, leading to degrees such as M.D. for a psychiatrist, Ph.D. or Psy.D. for a psychologist, M.S.W. for a social worker, or M.N. for a psychiatric nurse. While any well-trained practitioner in any of these disciplines can offer good, straight psychotherapy, each field offers certain special approaches. In looking at the differences between them, you should remember that the therapist's experience, rather than her qualifications, is probably the most important factor in determining how competent she is. Although a newly graduated psychiatrist may have eight or nine years of general and specialized medical training behind him, he does not have the solid background of experience in working with children that a psychiatric social worker with a great deal of child training and work experience can offer.

Psychiatrist

Psychiatrists are trained and licensed medical doctors (M.D.s) who specialize in the treatment of emotional disorders. Besides their general medical training, most psychiatrists have spent three or four postgraduate years providing full-time psychiatric treatment under supervision. Those wishing to specialize in child psychiatry spend two years treating and learning about children, and must pass special exams called "boards."

Because of their general medical background, psychiatrists are the only mental-health professionals qualified to prescribe medication. Their fees tend to be higher than others', due to the long training involved, but treatment with them or with licensed psychologists is automatically covered by health insurance when benefits include outpatient psychiatric treatment.

Clinical Psychologists

Clinical psychologists are professionals who have made a study of human behavior, development, and mental processes, and are trained to treat people with emotional disorders. After much early training within a doctoral program, the psychologist's internship involves at least a year of supervised practice at a hospital or clinic. A licensed psychologist has to have at least two years' supervised experience in providing treatment. A therapist has either a doctorate (Ph.D. or Psy.D.) or a master's degree (M.A. or M.S.), but requires a doctorate plus extra supervised experience in order to be licensed as a psychologist. These special requirements vary from state to state. Most psychologists are trained in a variety of approaches, such as various kinds of individual, group, and family therapy, even though they might specialize in only one. Some child psychologists have specialized, postgraduate training and supervised experience with children and parents, but there is no special license for child specialists as such. The psychologist is, in most states, the only mental-health professional qualified to do psychological testing.

Psychiatric Social Workers

Through the study of both sociology and psychology, psychiatric social workers are trained to understand how the psychology of the individual interacts with social and environmental issues. Training involves the equivalent of a year's supervised treatment experience practice, and results in a master's degree (M.S.W.) in social work. Two full-time years of supervised practice and the completion of an exam are required for certification by the Academy of Certified Social Workers (ACSW), but this certification doesn't mean that the person is experienced in therapeutic treatment. A psychiatric social worker specializing in child treatment may have completed a specialized postgraduate course or have extensive supervised work experience.

Most psychiatric social workers work in clinic settings, particularly with groups, or with families referred to social agencies, but many are in private practice. Their fees are not always covered by health insurers (clinic fees, on the other hand, are always covered).

Psychiatric Nurses

Psychiatric nurses are registered nurses (R.N.'s) with special training and experience in treating people in need of emotional help. They have completed a one- or two-year master's course in psychiatric nursing, including supervised practice, and have earned a master's degree (M.N., M.S., M.A., or M.S.N.).

Some psychiatric nurses working in private practice are certified by the American Nurses Association, which means that they have at least two years of supervised treatment experience and have passed an exam in either adult or child psychiatric nursing.

SETTINGS

There are a number of different settings for child therapy. Each has its benefits and its drawbacks, depending to some extent on where you live and what's available. The quality of treatment depends greatly on how good the facility is; in other words, a very good clinic can provide excellent treatment, surpassing what an inexperienced private therapist might be able to offer.

Private Therapy

The main advantage of private therapy is that you make the choice as to who treats your child. This choice encompasses not only the individual therapist, but also the approach that will be used. In other words, you can seek out a play therapist with a certain realm of experience (learning disabilities, for example) or a behavioral therapist experienced in the treatment of school phobia. For many parents, however, private therapy has the drawback of being more expensive than therapies in other settings.

If you would like your child to see a particular therapist but are not sure whether you will be able to afford her fees, it's worth discussing this with her; many private therapists offer reduced rates from time to time, depending on the individual case and on scheduling priorities.

Clinics

Clinics with mental-health services have the advantage of offering reduced fees, often on a sliding scale. Besides the financial benefits, you may prefer a clinic because a whole variety of services are offered; instead of your child being referred out for medication or family sessions, for instance, he will be able to receive these therapies within the clinic setting itself.

The disadvantage of any clinic is that, although you can certainly make a request, you might not be able to choose who will treat your child or which approach will be used. Nor can you be sure that the therapist will have specific experience in the area where your child's problems lie. Also, the person doing the initial evaluation or "intake" may not be the same person who will treat your child.

Clinics can be publically or privately sponsored, or attached to a community health center. Apart from these, the following might be available in your area:

University Psychology Departments. Almost every university with a graduate or doctoral program in clinical or school psychology will have a clinic set up for the purpose of providing psychologists in training with their first practical, supervised experience in treatment. The advantages and disadvantages are similar to those that apply to clinics.

Hospitals. Teaching hospitals have outpatient mental-health clinics where psychiatrists, psychologists, and social workers in training receive supervised experience in treatment. You might see a postgraduate student or a full-time professional; you generally have no choice in the matter. Non-teaching hospitals will often have an outpatient mental-health clinic with a permanent staff.

※

APPENDIX B:
OTHER FORMS OF
TREATMENT

Although this book focuses on play therapy, which is the area in which I work, there are other forms of treatment to which a play therapist sometimes refers parents, either during consultation or later. A therapist might recommend one or more of these forms either instead of individual psychotherapy or in conjunction with psychotherapy. She might be able to offer the treatment herself if it's just a matter of one or two sessions, and if she feels comfortable in the role, or she might refer you elsewhere for ongoing treatment. Let me briefly introduce you to the various options so that you can get a sense of how they work and when they might be appropriate.

FAMILY THERAPY

In family therapy, the individual child's problems are understood as symptomatic of difficulties within the family itself. For this reason, not only the child but also other family members, sometimes including grandparents or caretakers, all meet together with the therapist.

I will often recommend family therapy when I feel that a child's problems are the result of the ways in which various members of his family relate to or view one another. My treatment of an eight-year-old boy, for instance, involved occasional family sessions (concurrently with play therapy) in order to get total consensus about practical issues stemming from this boy's inability to accept the basic, day-to-day responsibilities with which life presented him. His parents had never asked very much of him in this area, and as a result he had been unable to develop a sense of himself as a competent individual. In discussing the problem as a family, together with their son, they were able to come to certain agreements about what kinds of demands it was reasonable to make of an eight-year-old boy, and how they could help their son to help himself.

Usually family work involves deeper psychological exploration. The family therapist tries to help various family members understand the ways in which they impact on one another. The therapist can also help the family understand how change for one member—from the loss of a job to the beneficial changes brought about by therapy itself—affects relationships within the family as a whole. Family therapists see this domino pattern of change as the family's way of maintaining a balance of personalities. If a mother, for instance, suddenly develops a new sense of independence when she starts working outside the home, another member of the family might become the "needy" one as a way of filling her slot.

Family therapy also deals with the ways in which a child's symptoms may serve a purpose in the makeup of the family— how, for instance, Johnny's tantrums deflect his parents' attention from their incessant fights, or how Sarah's school phobia is in fact her response to her mother's reluctance to let go of her "baby."

BEHAVIORAL THERAPY

Behavioral therapy does not seek to look inside the child in order to identify the cause of problematic symptoms, as does Play Therapy; instead, the behavioral therapist tries to erase the symptom itself, whether it's a phobia, bed-wetting, or some other specific, troublesome behavior. A good example of a simple behavioral approach that many parents are familiar with is the bell and pad system designed to help a child stay dry at night. Every time the pad gets wet, the bell rings and wakes the child. In time, the child learns to associate the need to urinate with waking up.

A behavioral approach is probably the best form of treatment for circumscribed problems—in other words, if the rest of the child's life is going well and the problem doesn't seem to be a symptom of some broader emotional upset. Very young children can easily become phobic, for instance, just through a single, frightening incident, and behavioral therapy can usually reverse this quickly and simply. On the other hand, when a child is older, phobias and bed-wetting problems are very often symptoms of a larger, emotional problem that needs a traditional, inside-looking approach like play therapy. In such a situation you should consult with a professional who can help you sort out whether or not this is a symptom of something more widespread.

If the picture is more complex, then the therapist might refer the child for a few sessions of behavioral treatment to work on the phobia, while she herself continues to work with the child on emotional issues; or she herself might be able to incorporate some behavioral work into her treatment of the child.

Cognitive-behavioral therapy is a form of behavioral therapy often used with children. It is particularly beneficial for impulsive children, as they are trained to stop and think rather than react automatically. Therapy is aimed at helping these children to develop self-control skills, and more reflective problem-solving strategies.

GROUP THERAPY

Group therapy for children is an important field, and one that is especially helpful for older children. It is often recommended in conjunction with individual treatment or, if individual treatment is not recommended, to deal with specific problems. It may be difficult to find an appropriate group for children, although many clinics and some schools run group sessions for kids, and there is a growing number of child group therapy courses being run around specific issues or themes—for instance, for children with severe fears, children of divorced parents or "blended" families, and children of alcoholic parents. These can be very useful in helping a child to get a broader picture of the situation he's in; it's always a relief to share a problem, to know you're not alone or all that different from many other children, and to see how others cope with similar issues. Through talk and play, children give one another support and help one another to find new ways of thinking about painful, shared experiences.

Other groups are oriented toward socialization problems. Being a member of a peer group is such a critical aspect of a child's development that group therapy can also be of great help to the child who's having trouble relating to other children. The group is almost like a laboratory setting in which the child can learn about himself in relation to others, and discover how to make things work better socially. By learning how to relate from watching other children in the group, and by providing feedback on how they experience one another, children help one another to learn social skills and to overcome specific problems such as shyness or bossiness. Additionally, groups and workshops are beginning to emerge around the country that teach overstressed kids how to relax and how to feel challenged rather than threatened by demands for achievement.

INFANT THERAPY

Infant psychotherapy (for children through the age of three) is a fast-developing, specialized field made possible by recent research into early emotional development, enabling trained professionals to spot potentially problematic interactions between parents and babies. According to pediatricians surveyed in a number of cities during 1989, 10 to 15 percent of infants brought to their offices had mild emotional problems that would benefit from short-term treatment. These problems included attachment disorders, withdrawal, sleep disorders, and irritability.

Infant therapy is really a variation of family therapy. Treatment nearly always involves parents in the sessions. The therapist watches parents and infant together in order to learn about the patterns of relating that have been building up between them, so that she can offer parents guidance on how to adapt to the needs of the small child. The mother of a very difficult baby, for instance, might need some help in adapting the way she responds to that baby's special needs.

DRUG THERAPY

Recent advances in psychological research have shown that certain disorders, such as hyperactivity and depression, are linked to biological factors. Children with these kinds of disorders have responded well to drug therapy using various forms of medication, alone or together with treatment. Many parents are familiar with Ritalin, for example, a medication widely used to treat hyperactivity. Antianxiety agents and antidepressants are also—but less frequently—prescribed for children.

Because medication can only be prescribed by a licensed psychiatrist, a nonmedical therapist would have to refer the child needing drug therapy to a psychiatrist with expertise in psychopharmacology.

PSYCHOLOGICAL TESTING

Psychological testing is a form of evaluation, not a form of treatment. It might be recommended during consultation with a therapist or in any situation where more needs to be known about a child, either by the therapist, by the school, or by parents themselves. A number of tests make up the "battery" of psychological tests. Each one is designed to gather fine-tuned information about a child's functioning in some specific area— personality tests, for instance, evaluate a child's emotional functioning through Rorschach and picture-story tests as well as others; intelligence tests evaluate his intellectual functioning; some tests can measure academic skills.

Taken together, these tests can help a professional sort out the ways in which various aspects of the child's functioning interact with one another. A child who has learning problems, for example, might be evaluated using personality and intelligence tests so that the therapist can establish whether his difficulties in the classroom are due to emotional troubles, poor visual or auditory functioning, a problem with memory or following directions, low intelligence, or a combination of several factors. For this reason, psychological testing is often recommended for children with learning problems.

Although it provides a very useful shortcut in learning about a child, psychological testing is used selectively by private therapists because it's a very costly and time-consuming process that must be carried out by a licensed psychologist. Clinics who have testers on staff, on the other hand, are much more likely to refer children for testing as part of the initial evaluation process.

INDEX

acting out, 29
action figures, 75
adolescence:
  as difficult phase, 11
  therapy for, x
adoption, 4
"aggressive threes," 11, 27, 30
alcoholism, 39, 214
anger:
  coping with, 27–28, 120
  of difficult children, 47
  divorce as cause of, 43
  drawings and, 90
  expression of, 20, 106–107, 125,
    139–140, 158, 165
  extreme, 19
  parental, 4, 120, 133, 134
  self-esteem affected by, 61, 65
  separation and, 8
  tantrums and, 88, 94
  verbalization of, 82, 103
animals, stuffed, 87
anxiety:
  ability and, 33
  bed-wetting and, 37
  coping with, 29, 33, 80, 99, 100, 105,
    162, 166
  drugs for, 215
  expression of, 82, 111, 194
  extreme, 15, 19
  high energy level vs., 15
  learning disabilities and, 116–117
  masturbation and, 39
  oppositional behavior and, 60

parental, 4, 5, 47, 127, 136, 143–
  144, 177, 178, 200, 202
reassurance and, 33
in relationships, 28–29
separation as cause of, 32–33, 125,
  140, 155, 174, 175, 201–202
therapy as cause of, 62, 63, 161, 164,
  165–166, 187–188
verbalization of, 102
apathy, 6
asthma, bronchial, 30
Attention Deficit Disorder, 57, 65
authority figures, 84, 189
autonomy, 25, 67, 123–124
avoidance, 105, 114, 136, 164, 184

baby-sitters:
  change of, 70, 152, 153, 171
  conflicts about, 4
  therapist's relationship with, 131, 194
baby talk, 16, 17, 127, 144
Barbie dolls, 75
bedtime, 17, 129
bed-wetting (enuresis), 23, 24, 37–38,
  60, 113, 136, 152, 172, 193, 213
behavior:
  abnormal vs. normal, 4–7
  activity level and, 144–145
  age-appropriate, 26
  aggressive, 11, 19, 22, 26–27, 58, 60,
    65, 144–145, 164, 180
  antisocial, 26, 34–35
  assertive, 203, 204
  censoring of, 93

context of, ix, 7
defensive, 162
disruptive, 20, 27, 58, 93, 106–107, 113, 135–136, 153, 155–156, 161–162, 197
infantile, 16, 107, 127
"naughty," 17–18, 20
negative consequences of, 108–109
obsessive-compulsive, 33–34
oppositional, 11, 12, 21, 25–26, 60, 95, 103, 106, 108, 112, 124–125, 155, 175, 179, 180
parenting skills for, 142
provocative, 183
ritual-bound, 33, 34
self-destructive, 72
selfish, 101
stabilization of, 180, 181
underlying problems in, 4, 6, 27
behavior modification, 179, 193, 213
birthday parties, 14, 31
birth history, 58
biting, 11, 22, 26
bossiness, 9, 27, 98, 99, 112, 169
bottle feeding, 16, 80, 112
building blocks, 82
bullying, 19, 21, 65

camps, day and sleepaway, 2, 100, 201, 203
cheating, 76, 184
child care literature, 142–143, 200
children:
    day-to-day experiences of, 138, 166, 177, 212
    decision-making by, 148–149
    difficult, 14, 46–48, 79–81, 112, 125
    divorce and, 41–44, 102, 109, 141, 164, 186, 193, 194, 196, 214
    egocentric thinking of, 111
    energy levels of, 15
    expectations of, 107, 109
    experience interpreted by, 15, 18, 19
    grieving by, 5–6, 40–41, 164
    imagination of, 83, 85
    individuality of, 5, 141–142, 174–175
    life-style of, 48–49, 81, 102–103, 150–151
    limited experience of, 111
    logic of, 15, 82, 110–112
    "magic rituals" of, 33, 34
    needs of, x, 146–148
    nurturing of, 78
    power struggles between parents and, 2, 3–5, 148–149
    pressured, 48–49
    risk factors for, 14, 39–49
    secondary caretakers for, 131, 139–140
    separation of mothers and, 8, 10–11, 12, 32, 51
    subjective experiences of, 15–16
    temporal sense of, 171

therapist's relationship with, 54–56, 65–66, 87, 92, 97, 108–109, 137–139, 154, 158, 164, 168, 170, 171–172, 178–179, 180–181, 183–184, 189–191, 192
compliments, 106, 108
confusion:
    in children, 19
    in parents, 4, 24, 136–137, 172
Connect Four game, 75, 115
constipation, 38
consultations, 50–73
    for babies and toddlers, 70
    about births of siblings, 52, 69, 72–73
    child-therapist relationship established in, 54–56, 65–66, 154
    child visits for, 51, 59–63
    for divorced parents, 40, 68, 71–72
    evaluation of therapist in, 53, 57–59, 200
    follow-up after, 73
    important issues discussed in, 53–54, 204
    note-taking in, 69
    one-time, 40, 49, 51, 69–70
    parent-therapist relationship established in, 52–54, 57–58, 186
    parent visits for, 50–51, 63–68, 118
    preparation of children for, 59–60
    preventative, 52, 69–70
    questions for, 53, 57–58
control:
    development of, 28, 120
    fear as basis of, 2
    in home vs. school, 6
    by parents, xi, 112, 125, 135, 141–142, 147, 148–149
    play as exertion of, 83–84
    tantrums and, 20, 23, 85–86, 93, 94, 96
    by teachers, 6, 33
coping:
    with anger, 27–28, 120
    with anxiety, 29, 33, 80, 99, 100, 105, 162, 166
    development of mechanisms for, 77–78, 94–95, 98, 99, 105–107, 109, 164, 168, 173–174
    with frustration, 27–28, 104, 130
    rational basis of, 106–107
    self-esteem and, 113–114
    with stress, 9–10, 62, 168, 174
couples therapy, 126, 127
creativity, 147
cursing, 95

day care, 41
denial, 63, 135–136
depression, 29–30, 144, 215
despair, 30, 174
development, 7–15
    change as part of, 5
    conflict in, 12

of coping mechanisms, 77–78, 94–95, 98, 99, 105–107, 109, 164, 168, 173–174
at different ages, 5, 11–12
emotional, 82, 95, 141, 165
equilibrium vs. disequilibrium in, 10, 11
fear of, 16
intellectual, 7, 22, 82, 85, 86, 102, 106–107
internal reorganization in, 11
natural, 177
normal problems in, 9–14
obstacles to, xi, 5, 8–10, 125, 162
oppositional behavior and, 26
phases of, 9, 11–12, 49, 135, 146
physical, 7, 14–15, 22, 85, 121
problems caused by, xi, 5, 8–10, 12, 21–22, 125, 162
progress in, 8, 177
regression and, 12, 15, 16–17
of relationships, 7, 58, 60, 65–66, 77–78, 80, 101, 107–109, 161, 163–164, 170–171, 174, 180–181, 183, 184
as "seesaw" process, 10–11, 174
of self-esteem, 7, 22, 34, 80–81, 112–117, 123–125, 196
of social skills, 7–9, 11–12, 22
stress and, 11, 12–14
diapers, 4, 8, 21, 143–144
diarrhea, 38
discipline, 3–4, 23, 44
discomfort, prolonged, 18–20
divorce, 41–44
    abnormal reactions to, 19
    aggressive behavior and, 27
    children affected by, 41–44, 102, 109, 141, 164, 186, 193, 194, 196, 214
    choosing sides in, 43
    custody and, 42, 132
    guilt as result of, 102
    normal reactions to, 6
    one-time consultation for, 40, 68, 71–72
    overcompensation in, 72
    parents affected by, 41, 71–72
    parent-work and, 131–132
    preparation for, 59, 67, 71
    remarriage after, 43–44
    separation and, 41, 71
    stress and, 12, 13, 39, 42, 43, 71
dogs, fear of, 18, 31
dolls, 75, 76–77, 81, 87, 88–89, 102–103, 150, 165, 166, 184
drawings, 90–91, 166, 172
dreams, 91
drug therapy, 215

eating problems, 4, 19, 29, 35, 36, 46
emotions:
    absence of, 40–41
    development of, 82, 95, 141, 165

expression of, x–xii, 28, 87, 99–100, 102–103
    false conclusions based on, 111
    "messes" from, 112
    negative, 179
    play as healthy for, 82–86
    verbalization of, 11, 81–82, 196
expeditions, 91–92

families:
    "blended," 214
    children's place in, 48–49, 81, 102–103, 150–151
    death in, 5–6, 13, 21, 39, 40, 52, 69–70, 133, 141, 152, 164, 167
    doll, 81, 102–103, 150
    dual-career, 17, 108, 139, 140
    illness in, 12
    over-scheduled, 48–49, 150–151
    problems in, 5–6, 23–24, 64, 66, 202
    tension in, 126–127
    therapy for, 202, 211–212, 215
    trips by, 2
    values of, 34, 35
fantasy, 35, 82–83, 84, 85, 87, 95
fathers, children's relationship with, 10–11, 32, 65, 182
fearfulness, 17–18, 25–26, 30, 114
frustration:
    coping with, 27–28, 104, 130
    of parents, 120, 130, 136
    toleration of, 11, 26, 146

genitals, preoccupation with, 38–39
group therapy, 213–214
guidance counselors, 135–136
guilt, 41–42, 102
    parental feelings of, 63, 64, 120, 130, 134, 135, 136, 137, 140

hair-pulling, 11, 26
handicaps:
    mental, 57
    physical, 39
headaches, 30
hitting, 11, 22, 26–27
home:
    behavior in school vs., 2–3, 6, 102
    environment of, 119, 122
homework, 25, 72, 92, 103–105, 114, 182
hospitals, 210
hyperactivity, 15, 147, 215
illness:
    exaggeration of, 121–122
    of parents, 12, 197, 198
    psychosomatic, 15, 29, 30
immaturity, 5, 6
infancy:
    difficult, 47, 70
    egocentricity of, 7, 8
    questions about, 58
    relationships developed by, 107, 146
    security of, 110
    therapy for, 214–215

irritability, 17, 46
irritable bowel syndrome, 30

jealousy, 113

kindergarten, 31, 74, 83

learning disabilities, 39, 44–46, 65,
    115–117, 141, 182–183, 209, 216
Lego blocks, 82, 85, 86
lying, 34–35

masturbation, 38–39
medication, 199, 215
mental retardation, 57
monsters, fear of, 18, 30, 60
moods, 4–5, 14
mothers:
    ability of, 134, 143–144
    over-dependency on, 51, 64–65, 110–
        111
    separation of children and, 8, 10–11,
        12, 32, 51
    working, 13, 41, 61, 89

nail biting, 17, 34
nightmares, 17, 37
noises, loud, 30
nursery school, 27–28, 31
nurses, psychiatric, 206, 208

obedience, 3, 4, 25
Oscar the Grouch doll, 76–77, 87, 88–
    89, 165, 184

panic, feelings of, 112
parents:
    adaptation by, 146–148
    alcoholic, 39, 214
    anger felt by, 4, 120, 133, 134
    anxiety felt by, 4, 5, 47, 127, 136,
        143–144, 177, 178, 200, 202
    arguments between, 97, 113, 126–
        127, 130, 139, 212
    attention of, 108
    avoidance by, 136
    biological, 68, 131, 132
    blame as concern of, 139–141
    childhood experiences of, xi, 127,
        130–131, 143–144
    confusion felt by, 4, 24, 136–137,
        172
    control by, xi, 112, 125, 135, 141–
        142, 147, 148–149
    decision-making by, 148–149
    demands by, 114–115
    denial by, 63, 135–136
    of difficult children, 47–48
    divorce and, 41, 71–72
    drug-dependent, 39
    expectations of, 6, 105
    failure felt by, 134, 135
    fear felt by, 64
    flexibility of, 49
    frustration felt by, 120, 130, 136

guilt felt by, 63, 64, 120, 130, 134,
    135, 136, 137, 140
hate felt by, 134
ideals of, 147
illness of, 12, 197, 198
insecurity felt by, 134
interviews with, 185–204
intuition of, 6, 153, 185–186, 199,
    204
irrational reactions by, 143, 144
limitations of, 53
limits set by, 3–4, 9, 24, 48, 63, 120,
    125, 140, 145–146, 147, 148, 188
listening by, 13
loyalty to, 44, 132, 198
as models, 130
permissive vs. strict, 143
power struggles between children and,
    2, 3–5, 148–149
problems as viewed by, 23–24, 133–
    137
punishment by, 17–18
separated, 24
shame felt by, 54, 63, 134, 137, 139,
    145
single, 17, 24, 48, 133–134, 164
step-, 68, 131, 132
styles of, x, 47, 124, 139, 140, 142–
    143, 144–146
support groups for, 126
tantrums and reactions of, 20, 136,
    152, 212
teacher's conferences with, 129, 142,
    153
tension between, 129–131
therapist's relationship with, ix–x,
    52–54, 57–58, 119, 122, 137–139,
    177–179, 181, 191–192
therapy and participation of, ix, 54,
    64, 67, 104–105, 137–141, 149,
    151, 164, 191, 195, 196
therapy for, 122, 126–128, 188–190,
    192, 194
parent-work sessions, 51, 118–158
    without child therapy, 122, 123–126
    commitment in, 118–119
    for divorced parents, 131–132
    effectiveness of, 142–151
    forms of, 122–132
    guidance in, 122, 124, 127, 150–151
    importance of, 74–75, 118–119
    individual parents consulted in, 129–
        131
    information exchanged in, 122, 137,
        142–143, 151–152, 154, 156–158
    note-taking in, 152
    painful feelings addressed in, 64,
        133–141
    parent-therapist relationship in, ix–
        xi, 52–54, 57–58, 119, 122, 137–
        139, 177–179, 181, 191–192
    phone contact in, 122, 124, 128, 129,
        152–153, 188
    as preventative measure, 121
    principles of, 119–122

privacy as issue in, 139
rights and responsibilities in, 154–158
schedule for, 122, 128, 142
self-awareness in, 142–144
typical session of, 128–129
utilization of, 151–153
pediatricians, 35, 142, 193, 215
peek-a-boo game, 82
personality:
  of child vs. therapist, 55
  external influences on, 127
  innate aspects of, 5
  maturing of, 16, 67
phobias, 18, 22, 30–32, 79, 80, 104, 105, 213
  of school, 31–32, 57, 148, 153, 174, 212
phone contact, 57, 73, 122, 124, 128, 129, 152–153, 188
piano lessons, 120–121
pica, 36
play, 81–89
  as compensation for wants, 84
  control exerted by, 83–84
  dates for, 19, 74
  emotional health promoted by, 82–86
  fantasy, 35, 82–83, 84, 85, 87, 95
  loss of interest in, 17
  reality reorganized in, 83, 86
  role-playing in, 83–84
  sense of mastery in, 85–86
  solitary, 29, 76, 78, 169
Play-doh, 86
play therapy, see therapy, play
politeness, 176
pre-schoolers, 5
problems, childhood, 18–39
  age-related, 21, 144, 146
  areas affected by, 21–23, 51, 64, 98, 101–102
  attention given to, 23, 137, 138
  in boys vs. girls, 20
  broad view of, 141–142
  current, 58
  developmental, xi, 5, 8–10, 12, 21–22, 125, 162
  duration of, 20–21, 24–25
  familial, 5–6, 23–24, 64, 66, 202
  genesis of, 67, 136
  intensity of, 20–21, 137
  isolated, 51, 59, 67, 69, 98, 123, 124, 213
  "normalization" of, 64
  parental reaction to, 23–24, 133–137
  physical health affected by, 22, 29–30, 47
  prevention of, 40
  signs of, 18–24, 42–43, 152–153
  socialization, 214
  temperamental, 124
  types of, 24–39
  unconscious conflicts in, 78–79, 80
  underlying, 4, 6, 27, 120
psychiatrists, 206–207
psychoanalysis, 57, 79, 179

psychological testing, 65, 215–216
psychologists, 206, 207
psychology departments, 210

recognition, 108
regression:
  births of siblings and, 72
  development and, 12, 15, 16–17
  in play therapy, 156, 165, 166, 172–176
  stress and, 16–17
relationships:
  adult, 108
  of adults and children, 32–33
  aggressiveness and, 11, 22, 26–27, 102
  anxiety in, 28–29
  cooperation in, 9, 11–12
  development of, 7, 58, 60, 65–66, 77–78, 80, 101, 107–109, 161, 163–164, 170–171, 174, 180–181, 183, 184
  of infants, 107, 146
  internalization of, 79
  rejection in, 105, 107
  self-esteem and, 114
  withdrawal from, 1–3, 14, 19, 28–29, 92
remediation, 182–183
report cards, 116
resentment, 113
responsibility, 120
restlessness, 17
Ritalin, 215
routines, rigid, 2, 129
rules, 85, 144, 148

sadness, 19, 27–28, 43, 99
school:
  academic achievement in, 15, 44–46, 115–117, 141, 216
  activities after, 120–121
  beginning of, 13
  behavior in home vs., 2–3, 6, 102
  classes after, 114
  concentration in, 13, 17, 22, 29, 40, 72, 155, 159
  disruptive behavior in, 20, 27, 58, 106–107, 113, 135–136, 153, 155–156, 161–162, 197
  phobia of, 31–32, 57, 148, 153, 174, 212
  referrals by, 54, 64, 135–136, 186, 201
  relationships formed in, 19, 101, 105
  unassertiveness in, 2
self-control, 145–146, 153
self-esteem:
  in adolescence, xii
  anger and, 61, 65
  anxiety and, 166
  birth of siblings and, 123, 124
  competence and, 22
  concrete skills and, 115
  coping mechanisms and, 113–114

development of, 7, 22, 34, 80–81, 112–117, 123–125, 196
of difficult children, 47–48, 79, 80–81, 112
learning disabilities and, 45, 46, 115–117
low level of, 20, 21–22, 23, 27, 75, 76, 85, 88–89, 93, 94, 98–101, 113, 163
lying and, 34, 35
mastery of tasks and, 45, 93–94, 104–105, 114–115
practical reinforcement of, 113–115
relationships and, 114
self-aggrandizement vs., 60–61
separation and, 67
shyness and, 50
separation:
in adolescence, x
anger and, 8
anxiety about, 32–33, 125, 140, 155, 174, 175, 201–202
death and, 69
dependency vs., 10–11, 22–23
divorce and, 41, 71
fear of, 19, 30, 31
feeling of weakness caused by, 3–4
of mother and child, 8, 10–11, 12, 32, 51
security and, 12
self-esteem and, 67
sleeping problems and, 36–37
stress and, 23
in therapy, 129, 169, 171, 181
toys used for, 78
sexual abuse, 39, 69, 153
shyness, 1–3, 14, 28–29, 50, 106
siblings:
birth of, 12, 13, 16, 19, 25, 27, 32, 40, 52, 69, 72–73, 123, 124, 187
individual temperaments of, 141–142
"silent cry," 40–41
sleeping problems, 4, 17, 22–24, 29, 35–37, 46–47, 51, 59, 101, 102, 126, 139, 176
sleepovers, 37
social workers, 199, 206, 208
soiling (encopresis), 38, 58, 97
spanking, 3, 139
spatial concepts, 82
special education, 197
speech therapy, 154
stealing, 34, 35, 153
stomachache, 30, 38
story books, 91
stress:
change and, 13–14
constitutional factors and, 14–15
coping with, 9–10, 62, 168, 174
development and, 11, 12–14
divorce and, 12, 13, 39, 42, 43, 71
fear and, 17–18
financial problems and, 13
illness and, 15
normal periods of, 12–13, 16–18

positive events and, 13–14
reactions to, xiii, 16–18, 24
regression and, 16–17
remarriage and, 44
signs of, 15, 16, 17–18
sources of, 12–14, 23
subjective responses to, 15–16
temperament and, 13, 14, 39
toleration of, 114–115
trauma as source of, 13, 39, 40–41
vulnerability and, 39
suicide, 30

tantrums, temper, 27–28
anger expressed by, 88, 94
causes of, 19–20, 138, 139
cessation of, 181–182
comfort for, 77, 93–95
containment of, 93–95, 151, 161
control as issue in, 20, 23, 85–86, 93, 94, 96
developmental necessity of, 11
duration of, 159
at home vs. school, 2, 74
limits set for, 9, 95–96
low self-esteem as cause of, 20, 21–22, 23, 75, 76, 85, 88–89, 93, 94, 113, 163
parents affected by, 20, 136, 152, 212
play therapy for, 74, 76, 88–89, 93–96, 165, 168, 172
triggers for, 65
uncontrolled, 147–148
verbalization vs., 28, 94–95
teachers:
control exerted by, 6, 33
difficult children and, 47–48
learning disabilities and, 116
as objects of blame, 20
parents' conferences with, 129, 142, 153
referrals by, 135–136
therapist's relationship with, 131, 155–156, 197, 199, 200
teasing, 114, 141
temperament:
of children vs. parents, 144–145, 147
"difficult," 14, 125
individual, 141–142
innate, 135, 137
as problem, 124
stress and, 13, 14, 39
"terrible twos," 11, 12, 21, 25, 26, 27, 30, 175
therapists, child:
billing system used by, 67
change of, 178–179, 186
child's relationship with, 54–56, 65–66, 87, 92, 97, 108–109, 137–139, 154, 158, 164, 168, 170, 171–172, 178–179, 180–181, 183–184, 189–191, 192
credentials of, 57, 192, 206–208
diagnosis by, 63–64
essential qualities of, 56

evaluation of, 53, 57–59, 200
experience of, 56, 57, 206
female vs. male, 56
flexibility of, x, 63, 191
judgment of, 53, 156–157
as neutral figures, 87, 95, 96, 108–109, 132, 138, 166, 194
as objects of blame, 140–141
one-time consultation with, 40, 49, 51, 69–70
parents' relationship with, ix–x, 52–54, 57–58, 119, 122, 137–139, 177–179, 181, 191–192
personality of, 55
physical appearance of, 55
psychological insights of, ix–x
questions asked by, 58, 61–62
recommendations by, 6, 53, 63, 120, 122, 124, 137, 150–151, 152, 154
referrals by, 122, 128
respect for, 155, 180–181
role of, 96–102
selection of, 205–210
teacher's relationship with, 131, 155–156, 197, 199, 200
theoretical approach of, 57
therapy, play, 74–117
activities used in, 89–92
adjustment in, 93
adult analysis vs., 79, 167
anxiety caused by, 62, 63, 161, 164, 165–166, 187–188
appointments for, 67, 154–155
case histories of, x–xi, 1–4, 6, 9, 19–20
child-therapist relationship in, 55, 87, 92, 97, 108–109, 137–139, 158, 164, 168, 170, 171–172, 178–179, 180–181, 183–184, 189–191, 192
in clinics, 186, 197, 198–199, 209–210, 216
confidentiality of, 57, 97, 129, 156–158, 186, 195, 198, 200
confused beliefs addressed in, 110–112, 167
consolidating phase of, 160, 168–169
control as issue in, 62, 76, 80, 98–99, 163, 170
coping mechanisms developed in, 77–78, 94–95, 98, 99, 105–107, 109, 164, 168, 173–174
course of action for, 64–66
definition of, 77–81
effectiveness of, 64, 186
emotions revealed by, x–xi
evaluation of, 177–181
exploratory phase of, 160, 164–168
fears addressed in, 77, 78
financial burden of, 57, 67–68, 69, 186, 196–197, 209
follow-up for, 182–184, 203
frequency of sessions for, 67
games used in, 75, 76, 85, 89–90, 115, 166, 168
goals of, 66, 179–180

as health decision, 155
internalization of, 168–169
introductory phase of, 80, 160, 161–164
laboratory setting for, 177
length of, 66–67
listening as important to, 97
long-term, 163
natural language of, x, 78–80, 82, 87
need for, 4–7, 18–24
as one form of therapy, 211–216
origins of, 78–79
parents' participation in, ix, 54, 64, 67, 104–105, 137–141, 149, 151, 164, 191, 195, 196
permission for, 67
phases of, 160–172
phone contact in, 57, 73
play as element in, 81–89
power struggles in, 115, 163
preventative, 40, 52
privacy as issue in, 156, 157, 185, 196
private practice for, 209
progress in, 156, 159–160, 162, 168–169, 170, 173–175, 177–179
psychoanalysis vs., 79, 179
psychological testing and, 65, 215–216
real-life issues in, 79
regression in, 156, 165, 166, 172–176
reintegration in, 107
rejection as issue in, 175–176
relationships developed in, 77–78, 107–109, 161, 163–164, 170–171, 174, 180–181, 183, 184
"remote-control button" used in, 61–62
resilience encouraged by, 176
resistance to, 92–93, 163
second opinions on, 177, 178–179, 180
self-awareness promoted in, 102–105
self-esteem developed in, 80–81, 112–117
self-revelations in, 61–62, 87, 89, 90, 95, 138, 161, 164–168
separation as issue in, 129, 169, 171, 181
settings for, 209–210
short-term, 62, 67, 189, 204, 215
termination of, 156, 160, 169–172, 175–176, 179–184, 186, 195
therapist's role in, 96–102
third-person therapy in, 87–89, 91, 99–100, 167, 184
toys used in, 75, 78, 82, 85, 87–89, 94–95, 165
trust established in, 77, 78, 97, 109, 156, 164–168, 174
understanding of, 74–75
verbalization in, 96–102
"weaning" from, 169, 171–172
see also consultations; parent-work sessions

thumb sucking, 16, 17, 34
tics, nervous, 17, 34
toddlers, 70, 146
toilet training, 5, 12, 16, 19, 21–22, 70,
    80, 110, 112, 126, 151
tutoring, 116, 154, 183

urination, excessive, 193, 194,
    195

verbalization, 96–102
    of anger, 82, 103
    of anxiety, 102
    of emotions, 11, 81–82, 196
    tantrums vs., 28, 94–95
violence, physical, 11, 22, 26–27
vulnerability, 39, 108

water, fear of, 31

9 780517 881699